I0139063

Justification

and the Call of the Gospel

George M. Ella

Go *publications*

Justification

Go Publications
The Cairn, Hill Top, Eggleston, Co. Durham, DL12 0AU, ENGLAND

© Go Publications 2011
First Published 2011

British Library Cataloguing in Publication Data available

ISBN 978-095486246-6

Printed and bound in Great Britain by Lightning Source (GB) Ltd

go *Topical*

Contents

Justification

Introduction

If God, in the justification of a sinner, merely accounts him righteous, and treats him as such, when, in reality, he is not so, then his judgment is not according to truth. But far be this from our God. Justice and judgment are the basis of his throne. He hath declared, that he will lay righteousness to the line, and judgment to the plummet. He will not in judgment either condemn the innocent or clear the guilty. If, therefore, he accounts any of Adam's race righteous, it is because he has first constituted them so.

It is with much pleasure I quote the sound words of Mr Hervey on this subject, in his letters to Mr John Wesley. The latter has asserted that "God, through Christ, first accounts, and then makes us righteous." To this Mr Hervey replies, "How? Does God account us righteous before he makes us so? Then his judgment is not according to truth. Then he reckons us to be righteous, when we are really otherwise. Is not this absolutely irreconcilable with our ideas of the Supreme Being, and equally incompatible with the doctrines of Scripture? There we are taught that God justifieth the ungodly. Mark the words. The ungodly are the objects of the divine justification. But can he account the ungodly righteous. Impossible! How then does he act? He first makes them righteous. After what manner? By imputing to them the righteousness of his dear Son. Then he pronounces them righteous, and most truly. He treats them as righteous, and most justly. In short, then he absolves them from guilt; adopts them for his children, and makes them heirs of his eternal kingdom."

Justification

Part One
Reformation and Counter-Reformation

Chapter 1

Biblical Justification and Counter-Reformation

The devil's counterfeits

The history of the Church of the Lord Jesus Christ is a history of reformation. The command she received from the Risen Lord was to go into all the world, preaching, baptizing, teaching and transforming that which sin had marred. The perpetual task of the Christian is to reform the world until the 'earth is full of the knowledge of the Lord, as the waters cover the sea', and all the elect are gathered in. The gospel which Christ gave His disciples, and which we have inherited, is a gospel of renewal, regeneration, rebirth and reformation. The devil, however, has always had his counterfeits and, whenever a work of God has been established, there has been a counter-reformation which has sought to destroy it. Wherever there has been a Peter or Paul to preach the truth, there has been a pope or a Simon Magus to bring in sacramentalism, formalism and the occult. Wherever a Wycliffe or a Bucer preached Christ, there was a Bishop Fleming or Cardinal Pole to dig up and scatter their bones in an effort to thwart the sowing of the good seed. Where the English Reformers taught the doctrines of grace, the papists introduced dogmas of works-righteousness and Jesuit deceit.

Not all counter-reformations were papist, however. Lutheran Joachim Westphal, supported Mary in preventing the exiled English

7

Justification

saints from landing on German and Danish soil. He called the brave English martyrs 'the devil's martyrs' and persecuted the Dutch, French and English Reformed churches with Anti-Christ-like fervour. The English Precisians and Disciplinarians fought the Elizabethan and Jacobean Reformers with their wish for a Parliament-run 'model church' with rigid, external forms, Continental vestments and intolerant laws. Whenever the great revivals of the European Continent, the British Isles and North America broke out in the seventeenth and eighteenth centuries, Rationalism, Arminianism, Grotianism, Latitudinarianism, New Divinity, Fullerism and Finneyism were there to offer stubborn combat.

Justification by faith challenged by modern 'Moderates'
Since the 1950s, there has been a deeper awareness amongst evangelical Christians of their duty to reform the world. At the same time, there has sadly been a strong resurgence of rationalistic teaching which has altered the general conception of what it means to be Reformed. For those who study in depth our 16th and 17th Century Reformers and compare the situation then with that of today, there is evidence in abundance to show that much of our present day Reformed Establishment, with all its eagerness to reform, is counter-reformed in thought, word and deed. Indeed, what was called the Reformed Establishment in the fifties, sixties and seventies of last century with its emphasis on justification and imputed righteousness appears to have become just another Liberal section of institutionalized Christianity with its roots in the so called rights of man. Thus, modern contenders for this pseudo-Christianity such as Erroll Hulse, preach faith in Christ as a human right. Ironically enough, Hulse runs a magazine called 'Reformation Today', which has as its object to denounce the Reformation of Jewel, Latimer, Grindal, Lever, Coverdale, Bucer, Bullinger and Calvin who all emphasized the active work of God's grace in salvation. It has been replaced by a wishy-washy theory of man's endeavours to get his act together and better himself through a period of Adam-like probation so that with man doing his all and God doing His all, both sides are reconciled. This author recognizes that such a theology is shameful and blasphemous and pretends to lift man to a position he can never

gain because of his sin. Rather than view man as on probation and one who might yet make the grade, we must view him as a miserable, lost sinner who has no means in himself to raise himself from the condemnation that is justly his. It is thus of vital importance that we continually renew our knowledge and experience of what Reformation is all about and critically compare today's evangelical teaching with that of the Scriptures and God-chosen leaders in Reformation times who rescued their flocks from papist superstitions. Such a study will show that though there is a welcome stress on preaching and evangelism in today's nominally Reformed churches, the doctrines of the Reformation have again disappeared so thoroughly that we must conclude that we are, once again, in dire need of a Reformation.

Undoubtedly, the key slogan of the Reformation was 'Justification by Faith'. Equally without a doubt, our Reformers had a decretal, predestinarian, Christo-centric, saving, man-transforming view of such a justifying faith, whereas most modern Reformed believers today have slid back into either papist, Pelagian, Arminian or Fullerite ways of works-righteousness or else look upon justification as a mere legal fiction. Thus, justification is now described widely, when it is discussed at all, either as a reward, couched in terms of rights or prerogatives of the sinner gained through accepting invitations or exhortations to exercise his duties to God as if he had never sinned, or else a mere forensic change of status which secures pardon for a sinner but does not change him or remove his guilt.

A lethal, legal belief
However, another old Counter-Reformation belief has again become fashionable, combining the two views outlined above. We need a double justification or double righteousness, we are told. The first is a mere sinecure status, termed quite falsely 'legal righteousness'. This is a preliminary declaration of righteousness on God's part in terms of status rather than state. Thereafter, we need what is equally erroneously called 'evangelical righteousness'. Here justification is seen from the point of view of man's agency and contribution. This is his personal sanctification and Christian walk which places him in the state of justification. Together, and only together, these two kinds of

Justification

justification make a man truly righteous and meet for the status and state of being fully justified. Such is the lethal, legal belief.

Many modern pseudo-Reformed thus do not look upon justification as the culmination of being set right with God but as the first step in a justifying life of faith, producing repentance and sincere obedience. Though there is obviously a place for both these virtues in the Christian life, neither precedes justification nor earns it. Sadly, few Reformed leaders today tell us that justification and faith are solely God's prerogatives, ordained and given in eternity to His elect. Few teach, as our Reformers, that justification is God's elective decree, that faith is a demonstration of Christ's faith imputed to the believer and that the Spirit's sovereign work is to enlighten from within and present the justified and faithful ones before the world and the judgment throne of God as Christ's redeemed. Indeed, modern counter-reformers tell us that such teaching smacks of Hyper-Calvinism and Antinomianism. It is thus to be regarded as a downgrading of true religion when William Twisse, the great defender of Reformation doctrines and a staunch believer in justification from eternity, is attacked in a recent 'Reformed' publication for believing in justification given to the ungodly which brings Christ's faith to the sinner but is not the result of the sinner's faith.[1] Yet the only way to have peace with God is through His justifying mercies. There can be no preaching of the gospel, no call to repent and believe the gospel, indeed, no gospel at all without clear Biblical teaching on justification. The call of the gospel is not a gospel call if the sinner is not told how he can become right with God i.e. the doctrine of justification.

Biblical justification sold as Hyper-Calvinism and Antinomianism
Clarity concerning the two terms 'Hyper-Calvinism' and 'Anti-nomianism' must be gained in order to understand the modern doctrinal dilemma and growing aversion to the old Reformed paths. The Reformers knew no such teaching as 'Hyper-Calvinism', nor do modern users of the term define or apply it in any meaningful or even generally valid way. Like many words used for mere rhetoric effect, it appears to be empty of semantic content. We find a typical example of

---

[1] *Justification Vindicated*, BOT, 2002. See the editor's negative comment "Twisse unfortunately asserted that justification is from eternity", to a positive remark by Robert Traill, p. 24.

the confusion associated with the term in Kenneth G. Talbot's and W. Gary Crampton's joint work *Calvinism, Hyper-Calvinism and Arminianism.*[2] The authors never seem to be sure where they stand in relation to their three subjects, though they claim to be Calvinists to the core. The authors' preface informs the reader that "Hyper-Calvinism, as the name implies, is a perversion of Calvinism. It so stresses the sovereignty of God that man's responsibility is practically eliminated." Yet, in chapter nine, 'Is God the author of Sin?', the authors stress the sovereignty of God so much that they rule out any responsibility of man both in the matter of his fall and the matter of his salvation. Indeed, they affirm dogmatically that God has decreed sin for His own glory. The authors give Ephesians 1:11 and Romans 11:33, 36 as their 'proof' for this allegation. The two passages say:

> In whom also we have obtained an inheritance, being predestinated according to the purpose of him who worketh all things after the counsel of his will,

and,

> O the depth of the riches both of the wisdom and knowledge of God! How unsearchable are his judgments, and his ways past finding out! For who hath known the mind of the Lord? Or who hath been his counsellor? Or who hath first given to him, and it shall be recompensed unto him again? For of him, and through him, and to him, are all things: to whom be glory for ever. Amen.

One must ask what these fine expressions of grace have to do with a God who decrees sin? Furthermore, in their wider definition of Hyper-Calvinism on pages 76 and 77 of their work, Talbot and Crampton tell us that in this dogma "The secret will of God is so accentuated, that the revealed will is de-emphasised." Surely to account for sin being in the world at God's decree is to exercise dogmatic speculation into the secret will of God which is not backed

---

[2] Still Waters Revival Books, 1990.

11

Justification

up by God's revelation expressed by the authors' alleged Scriptural evidence. Furthermore, in the very same chapter, the authors quote Augustine who maintained that sin is the absence of God's will, occurring where God's will is not recognized. However, according to Talbot and Crampton, sin is obedience to God's will, which many would claim is an extreme Hyper-Calvinist dogma. Most modern so-called 'Moderate Calvinists' argue that the Hyper-Calvinist refuses to preach the whole gospel to all men everywhere.[3] However, when one examines their gospel, it is a cut down system which quite rules out the preaching of the doctrines of grace which they maintain would confuse the unconverted sinner and therefore should only be preached to believers.

Andrew Fuller, rightly censured for his un-Biblical doctrine of the atonement by James P. Boyce in his *Abstract of Systematic Theology*, is praised in a recent Banner of Truth foreword to a reprint of Bunyan's *Come and Welcome to Jesus Christ* for his *The Gospel Worthy of All Acceptation*, viewed by the publisher as freeing the churches from the grip of Gill's alleged Hyper-Calvinism.[4] Apparently the Banner will have us believe that Bunyan's sermon reflects Fuller's theology. However, Bunyan gives the lie to Fuller's wayward teaching regarding the atonement, reconciliation, imputed righteousness, law, gospel, justification and the believer's eternal security. Indeed, Bunyan's two major works on the law and justification, dealt with when we come to discuss his faith in more detail below, are a point by point refutation of the ideas disseminated by Fuller and his modern followers, especially their views of law and grace. The publisher says Fuller "was raised under a ministry which had become unbalanced due to its Hyper-Calvinist emphases" as if he were innocent of its teaching and had not taught the same doctrines himself. The fact that Fuller pastored Soham for several years and never gave up a number of these 'emphases', such as his insistence that the full gospel was for believers only, is suppressed. So too is the fact that Fuller was responsible for leading the church into Socinianism. On the other hand, Gill was never part of the Hyper-Calvinistic system and

---

[3] See Phillip R. Johnson's article in Sword & Trowel for March 2002, A Primer on Hyper-Calvinism, p. 12.
[4] BOT, 2004.

preached repentance and faith to all throughout his far more successful ministry. The myth that Gill lagged behind Fuller in exhorting the sinner to turn to God is exploded by Gregory Wills in his fine essay *A Fire that Burns Within: the Spirituality of John Gill*.[5] Indeed, in the same volume Tom Nettles claims Gill "sang in unison" with Whitefield. Who would honestly deny (except the Banner of Truth) that Gill stood far closer to Bunyan than Fuller? Indeed, in striving to secure themselves on both sides from adverse criticism, much of our modern Reformed Establishment has resorted to the surprising artifice of adopting both.

Antinomianism

The term 'Antinomian', has also lost any generally valid meaning and become a mere protest slogan against old orthodoxy. It was initially used by our Reformers to mean those "who will not have God's law to be preached, nor the consciences of sinners to be terrified and troubled with the judgments of God".[6] It has become fashionable for many well-known Reformed party, men of the present day to exclude our pioneer Reformers and Puritans and men of the 17th Century Awakening such as Crisp, Twisse, Skepp, Romaine, Hawker, Gill, Brine, Hervey, Toplady, Ryland Sen. and Huntington from their list of doctrinal heroes for the unfounded reason that they were 'Antinomians'. These men were demonstrably more industrious in preaching the terrors of the law than their modern critics and far less Antinomian. The charge of Antinomianism falls back on those who break the commandment "thou shalt not bear false witness". Indeed, on reading how the anonymous Banner of Truth (BOT) publisher of their version of Bunyan's famous work mentioned above misleads his readers by pretending that Fuller and Bunyan held to the same Counter-Reformation theology, one could only use a favourite cliché of theirs "Antinomianism without a mask".

Our modern criers of 'Antinomian' tend on their part to preach a natural, common grace law which puts believers and unbelievers alike under the same grace. It holds no initial terrors for the sinner but is seen as an encouragement to keep the Mosaic law by natural duties

---

[5] *The Life and Thought of John Gill*, ed. Michael Haykin, Brill, 1997.
[6] Rogers' *Exposition*, p. 92.

Justification

and to accept the saving revelation of God by a process of logical deduction based on them. Every law of God, they tell us, teaches us to accept God's entire revelation and the more the law is followed, the more we shall learn to love the law and the Saviour to whom it points. Only when this is rejected by a sinner fitted out with the natural abilities to understand what is going on will he be faced with judgment for not hearkening to a saving grace offered to all. Thus the law to them is a way of salvation and not the divine way of condemnation followed by our Reformers to pronounce man guilty and reveal to him his total depravity and lost state before God. Their evangelists and pastors are told that they must woo sinners to Christ and not scare them by holding up the condemning mirror of the Mosaic law before their polluted souls. Sinners are merely told to love Christ as if they had never apostatised.[7] "Love Christ because Christ loves you all", is their parole. This is Antinomianism at its most deceptive and a total misuse of the law.

Secondly, our Reformers looked on Antinomians as those "which think the outward calling by the word, a sufficient argument of their election unto life."[8] Now none of those orthodox men whom our modern common-grace, duty-faith, pseudo-Reformed brethren call 'Antinomians' believed such a doctrine. However, those who so soon cry 'Antinomian' of others are, by their own definition, Antinomians themselves. It is they who say that the atonement was made for every man and the saving call goes out to every man and Christ is freely offered to every man, thus equating the outward call of the gospel with Christ's saving intention for every individual. Here, we can call John Murray as a witness who concludes his BOT reprint entitled *The Free Offer*, with the words:

> The full and free offer of the gospel is a grace bestowed upon all ... the grace offered is nothing less than salvation in its richness and fullness. The love or loving-kindness that lies back of that offer is not anything less; it is the will to that salvation.

---

[7] Following Fuller, *Works*, Vol. ii, pp. 375, 376.
[8] Rogers' *Exposition*, p. 152.

'Antinomianism' has become the rallying call for retreat
Sadly those who are eager to introduce new systematic and dogmatic theories nowadays are fleeing more and more from healthy theological debate by calling all those who will not accept their new idea for good old reasons 'Antinomians'. These critics invariably overlook the sound experimental heart religion of those with whom they disagree and judge them by their own criteria, dissecting their brethren's views as a butcher cuts up a sheep's carcass. They soon lose the sheep in the pile of mutton! There is a sad example of this kind of confusion in *Justification Alone* issued by a team of writers of various views and edited by Don Kistler.[9] In chapter 3, Dr Joel Beeke deals with the question of the relationship of faith to justification but stumbles over the old question of which came first, the hen or the egg. He is sure however, that he must reject the 'Antinomian' teaching of Abraham Kuyper, William Gadsby and J. C. Philpot.[10] Hitherto in my readings of modern protagonists of the solely forensic as opposed to the declarative and the heart-experience view of justification, I have noticed that Kuyper has been used and misused repeatedly *against* so-called Antinomians. Now he is called an Antinomian himself for believing in the fact that the elect are justified by God from eternity and in the resurrection of Christ and that when faith comes to a sinner, he is made conscious of what Christ has done for him. This is a most surprising statement as this is the view of most of our early Reformers from which our modern pseudo-Reformed men seem to have departed. After all, from whence would we expect God to act apart from in eternity where He dwells and how else would we expect Him to reveal His mercies but in time through the gift of faith leading to a conscious awareness of the fact? Dr Beeke surely errs even more in saying that Gadsby, Philpot and "most of the Strict Baptists" hold that "the believer is justified in time only with respect to his own conscience by the Spirit's witness." Now this does not sum up the entire, well-balanced teaching of these two men at all as their writings on justification plainly show. One of the most beautiful essays one can possibly read on the subject is Gadsby's *What is Faith?* In this work,

---

[9] Soli Deo Gloria, 1996.
[10] Op. cit., p. 95.

Justification

Gadsby relates how sinners are to be wooed and won for Christ and he takes the reader step by step through the conversion experiences of Biblical characters emphasizing the work of the Spirit melting the stony heart of the sinner. Only after this work of God is accomplished can the sinner say in retrospect, "When faith receives the glorious truths of the atonement and righteousness of Christ, then the soul can sweetly exclaim, 'In the Lord have I righteousness and strength'."[11] We must note, too, that Gadsby is writing in criticism of Sandemanianism which was all head doctrine and no heart and feelings. Gadsby points out to William Stephens that Sandemanianism's denial of the believer's union with Christ from eternity puts them off the Biblical track of justification and faith. He is faithful to the gospel by informing his opponent that God has blessed His people with all spiritual blessings in heavenly places in Christ according as they were chosen in Him before the foundation of the world (Ephesians 1:3 ff.) so that the man of God may be "thoroughly furnished unto all good works". He is thus quite in keeping with gospel truths in affirming that in matters of faith, man has nothing to bring to merit it, but nevertheless receives all as a free gift.

Contrary to Dr Beeke's animadversion in reducing Philpot's doctrine of justification to a mere influence on the conscience by the Spirit, even though that belief is, in spite of Dr Beeke's criticism, Biblical and thus honourable, Philpot maintains: "I consider the doctrine of the believer's justification through the obedience of Christ imputed to him for righteousness, to be one of the greatest importance and could not unite with anyone who denies it."[12] Of course, Philpot, like Gadsby, did object to those Reformed dogmatic theorists who viewed theology as a series of logical postulates and axioms void of heart-religion. He also criticised those who felt they could get to Mount Zion without first going to Mount Sinai. They invariably found that their Zion was indeed Sinai. Here, again, Philpot stood firmly on the shoulders of the Reformers. He was also fully reformed in his conviction that justification endued the former sinner with true heart-religion. Scoffers used to ask him how he came to believe that God

---

[11] *Works of William Gadsby*, J. Gadsby, 1847, p. 298. The entire essay should be studied carefully in order to comprehend the full origin, purpose and extent of God's gift of faith.

[12] *The Seceders*, Farncombe and Sons, Vol. II, p. 144.

justified sinners as sinful sinners and not as godly sinners and he would give his own testimony by way of reply. This rattled his critics as they wanted abstract theological (or rather philosophical) propositions and conclusions rather than the empirical, first-hand facts. He told these 'holier than thou theorists', that he would have been able to fellowship with them better if they showed "more experience and less doctrine, more confession of ignorance and less assumption of knowledge, more of the spirit and less of the letter, more of the Creator and less of the creature."[13]

Believing because of justification or believing to be justified?
Dr Beeke cannot accept that faith on coming to Paul and the Apostles gave them the assurance that they were already justified. He argues in contrast that they came to Christ *that they might be justified*. The difference is, according to Beeke, that his 'Antinomians' believe in justification from eternity whereas justification must be viewed as coming after faith i.e. one comes in faith to Christ that one might be justified. Thus faith must be prior to justification and is a righteous work procuring justification. Beeke provides Galatians 2:15, 16 as evidence but this is surely ill-chosen as these verses clearly show that it is Christ's faith which justifies and not the sinner's own. Paul gives ample testimony in the following verses that justification is not by means of personal faith demonstrated by one classified in Scripture as 'ungodly' or God's 'enemy' but by the fact that Christ had already redeemed them from the curse of the law (which is a synonym for justification) and that the reception of Christ's faith was a covenantal decree of God's before even the law was instituted and that in applying faith to the elect, Christ is carrying out His eternal role as Mediator. As Bunyan taught in his *Justification by an Imputed Righteousness*,[14] the sinner's righteousness resides in Christ, reserved for His people and that the imputation of that righteousness to the elect was a foregone conclusion before ever Paul and the Apostles came on the earthly scene. He also stresses that it was Christ's obedience 'long ago' that justified the elect. In other words, the faith given to Paul and the Apostles was not *so that they might be justified*

---

[13] Ibid, p. 145.
[14] Offor's edition, Vol. I, p. 300 ff.

17

Justification

but it was given them so that they might recognise their justification and accept the finished work of Christ in their lives. Indeed, Bunyan argues in the section marked *Men are justified from the curse of the law before God while sinners in themselves* that when Christ fulfilled the righteousness of the law, he fulfilled it in all the elect. Thus when faith comes to the elect, it comes, in Bunyan's words, to make God's mercies sure to the soul. They find out what God has already done for them. This theme is again taken up in Bunyan's *A Defence of the Doctrine of Justification*. When faith comes to a sinner, it is with the conviction given him, that though he is a sinner, he has already been reconciled to God and is given to believe that there is a righteousness already completed for him. Faith does not tell a sinner that *this might be* the case but that *it is*. Thus faith is not a procuring cause of justification but an application for the justification already made (Romans 5:9, 10; Colossians 1:20; Ephesians 4:32).[15] Both Gadsby and Philpot would be the first to claim that those who do not see the object of their faith as being in the sure and certain mercies of God sealed in the blood of Christ and reserved for the elect sinner long before their acquaintance with them have much to learn in the school of Jesus.

In the light of Gadsby's and Philpot's defence concerning the experimental nature of justification, it is most worrying to find Dr John Armstrong in his chapter on *The Sufficiency of Faith for Justification* in the same book wrenching Bunyan out of his context to prove his, not Bunyan's, doctrine that "This righteousness of faith is not a quality seen within our hearts, or felt by us experimentally".[16] On reading these wayward words, Philpot would have immediately pointed Armstrong to the Joseph Hart hymn he and his people loved so well:

> Let us ask the important question,
> (Brethren, be not too secure),
> What it is to be a Christian,
> How we may our hearts assure.

---

[15] Ibid, Vol. II, p. 295.
[16] *Justification by Faith Alone*, pp. 157, 158

Vain is all our best devotion,
If on false foundations built;
True religion's more than notion,
Something must be known and felt.

Bunyan clearly states in *Justification by an Imputed Righteousness*, the book from which Armstrong carelessly quotes and places in a foreign context, that righteousness belongs to Christ alone but when this righteousness is imputed to the believer, he the believer becomes aware of the many wonderful ways grace works in his heart. After all, he no longer has a heart of stone.[17] Armstrong will not have this. It is confusing justification with regeneration and sanctification, which is a Roman error, he says. Gadsby, Philpot and Bunyan however argue, in keeping with the great Reformation cloud of witnesses, that justification is inseparable from regeneration, sanctification and the indwelling of the Spirit. They admit that they can be separated on the dissecting table of systematic theology but not in practice and Christ's righteousness is a very practical, transforming matter.

Amyraldism and Neonomianism responsible for wrong views on justification

Most major revolts against the Reformation in Britain from within the Reformed churches arose during the middle of the 17th Century. These were caused by Amyraldism and Neonomianism, two forms of universalism condemned by our Reformers. The term Amyraldism is derived from the name of Moses Amyrald (1596-1664), a French lecturer at Saumur who strove to re-interpret the Canons of Dort. These canons had been drawn up with the close co-operation of the Church of England who were satisfied that they conformed to the Thirty-Nine Articles. Amyrald, strove to rid them of their Reformed content and re-interpret them as a half-way house to Arminianism, though he was an opponent of full Arminianism. Christ has indeed

---

[17] The exact source, which Armstrong does not give, is found in Offor's edition, Vol. 1, p. 302. I have outlined the correct context of Bunyan's statement towards the end of my more detailed study of Bunyan's doctrine in Part 2, Chapter 2: Seventeenth Century Puritans.

Justification

died for all men, Amyrald taught, but only on condition that they believe. Thus the atonement was hypothetically for all but merely applicable to some. The sinner who thus rejects Christ, breaks the effectiveness of the atonement, making it null and void for him.

Amyrald's views, however, on examination, are those of his lesser known tutor, John Cameron, who introduced a system of universal atonement to reconcile predestination with common grace, which he called 'universal grace'. He was ably met by Bishop John Davenant, one of the most important pillars of the Synod of Dort who pointed out in his *The Judgment of Bishop Davenant* that the logical meaning of Cameron's words was Semi-Pelagian and that what he called 'universal grace' was the 'common philanthropy' of God which had nothing to do with saving grace.[18] J. L. von Mosheim, no extremist by any means, mentions that there are those who believe the Cameron-Amyrald teaching reflects a true understanding of the Reformed faith but such apologists have merely a "desire of softening certain Reformed doctrines, which afforded to the papists as well as to others much occasion of reproach" and comments further:

> But I doubt whether such persons have duly considered both the principles from which it is derived and the consequences to which it leads. After considering and reconsidering it, it appears to me to be Arminianism, or, if you please, Pelagianism artificially dressed up and veiled in ambiguous terms; and in this opinion I feel myself confirmed when I look at the more recent disciples of Amyraut, who express their views more clearly and more boldly than their master.[19]

The fact that jumbled thinking and lack of clarity amongst Amyraldians appears to be a mark of the error is illustrated by the large correspondence in the contemporary Christian press between Dr Alan Clifford's presentation of Amyraldians and those who strive to

---

[18] See Morris Fuller's excellent analysis with Davenant's full reply in *The Life of Bishop Davenant*, Chapter IX, On the Gallican Controversy.

[19] *Mosheim*, Murdock twelfth edition, p. 817.

confute him who are more markedly Amyraldian than he in their arguments, nearly all sides professing to be 'Reformed'.

Against this teaching, it must be said that an atonement which only takes on its meaning when accepted, is neither objectively sufficient for all of itself or even objectively effective for a limited number. The limited effectiveness of the Amyraldian system does not lie in the nature of the atonement itself but in the acceptability of the believer. Such a view denies that Christ atoned for those placed in union with Him before the foundations of the world, and those only, and destroys thus the Biblical doctrine of election. An atonement that has no respect to particular persons stands in sharp contrast to the words of Christ who died knowingly for His elect sheep and was a sacrifice for their sins (John 10:11, 15, 26, 28; John 17:9, 19; Titus 2:14).

Moreover, according to Scripture, it is the death of Christ itself that removes condemnation and not the mere application of that death (Romans 8:32, 34). Furthermore, an atonement which the sinner can opt out of at will throws a very negative light on the sovereign will of God in designing that atonement. The Bible teaches, in contrast, that it was whilst we were in opposition to God, even enemies of God, that Christ's atoning and reconciling death became effective for us (Romans 5:10; 2 Corinthians 5:19; Ephesians 2:13, 16, 17; Colossians 1:20, 22). This goes also for justification (Romans 4:5, 25).

Neonomianism
A further group to be found in our Reformed circles who have rejected the teaching of the Reformers are the Neonomians who follow Richard Baxter in bringing in a new form of Arminian legalism. As modern Reformed works, for obvious reasons, soft pedal on Neonomianism as they do on Amyraldism, we resort to quoting Louis Berkhof's 1937 work originally called *Reformed Dogmatics*, republished in 1949 as *The History of Christian Doctrine* and reissued in 1969 by the Banner of Truth Trust. Berkhof says on page 192:

> The name (Neonomianism) is due to the fact that it practically changed the Gospel into a new law. According to this view Christ atoned for all men in the sense that He made salvation possible for all, and thus

Justification

brought them into a savable state. He met all the conditions of the covenant of works, and thereby abrogated the old law of that covenant, so that His work can be called our legal righteousness. Having met all the conditions of the covenant of works, He then introduced a new law, the law of the Gospel, which requires faith and conversion. These constitute the evangelical righteousness of the believer which, however imperfect it may be, is the ground of his justification rather than the imputed righteousness of Jesus Christ. Thus the covenant of grace was changed into a covenant of works. This is simply Arminianism under a new name.

Donald G. Davis concluded his *Baker's Dictionary of Theology* entry on Amyraldism with the words "Amyraldianism lives on, however, in much of modern Calvinism". Sadly, this can also be said of Neonomianism. It is interesting to note that it is the Neonomian, pseudo-Reformed who so often use the term 'Antinomian' against those they oppose. 'Antinomian' would thus mean 'Anti-Neonomian' and backfires on its users. Neonomianism is pure Counter-Reformation theology which leads the holder swiftly back to Rome. Particularly Roman is the Neonomian belief that justification is based on the double footing of Christ's atonement and man's endeavours. It has thus become something of a slogan in various Reformed circles to stress that salvation is all of God and all of man.[20] Henry Bullinger, whose works were the widest read of any Continental theologian in England for well over a hundred years and officially endorsed compulsory reading for the clergy, condemned this watered down version of Reformed doctrine in his Second Helvetic Confession, stating:

> Therefore, we do not divide the benefit of justification, giving part to the grace of God or to Christ, and part to ourselves, our charity, works, or merit; but we

[20] See Iain Murray's *Spurgeon v. Hyper-Calvinism*, p. 84; Geoffrey Thomas, Evangelical Times, July 1995, p. 11.

do attribute it wholly to the praise of God in Christ, and that through faith.[21]

The attempt to depict God and man as co-workers in redemption finally brought Genevan theology to its knees. Francis Turretin (1623-1687), the last of a long line of Calvinist leaders in the city-state, drew up the *Formula Consensus Helvetica* which was designed to protect the Reformed faith from several major errors in Saumur teaching. The *Consensus* condemns outright the Amyraldian and Neonomian views of a universal atonement and the doctrine that God desires the salvation of all yet does not will to accomplish it. However, when Jean Alphonse Turretin (1674-1737) took over from his father, he welcomed the Saumur teaching with open arms and, as G. P. Fisher so aptly puts it in his *History of Christian Doctrine*, Alphonso 'was as zealous in opposing (the *Consensus*) as his father had been in advocating it.'[22] Needless to say, Turretin Jnr. maintained that his was the original and true teaching of the English Reformers. Papist theologians were delighted at Alphonse's climb-down and the Jesuit François de Pierre boasted in a work published in 1728 that Alphonse Turretin's new theology took the Reformed church back into the bosom of Rome.

History has thus left us nowadays with Reformed churches which are such in name only and which hover between the doctrines of our Reformers and those of Rome. Though they claim to preach the true Reformed faith for today, their true slogan is 'Counter-Reformation Today!' Even the staunchest professing Calvinists appear to have great difficulty in defining their faith in truly Reformed and Biblical concepts nowadays. Again, we can use the work of Talbot and Crampton as a modern example of this modern inability to think in a clearly Reformed way. In spite of their ambiguity on Hyper-Calvinism, they sometimes come up with fine statements of the Reformed position such as their summary of Calvinism on page 76:

---

[21] See Beeke and Ferguson, *Harmony of Reformed Confessions*, 1999, p. 100.
[22] See section *Modern Theology*, pp. 345, 346.

Justification

> Our study has also revealed that the Lord Jesus Christ died an atoning death for the elect of God. His sacrificial work was only for the elect. Those whom the Father has chosen, and for whom the son has died, are drawn irresistibly to Christ by the Father. They are called into union with the Son.

Yet in their fifth chapter, 'The Atonement of Christ', they present a quite different view. Here, they do not claim that Christ's "sacrificial work was only for the elect" but that "Calvinism avers that the atonement of Jesus Christ was *sufficient* to save all men." We are further told that the atonement was not *efficient* enough for this purpose so that only the elect are redeemed. This is truly Amyraldian and Arminian in content. The authors claim as Calvinism, and therefore the Reformed faith, the theory of a universal atonement which is effective in some cases and ineffective in others. What a strange view of our immutable and Sovereign God is presented here! God designs an atonement which does not work. For an atonement to be sufficient, it must be sufficiently effective to attain its purpose. It must be sufficient to perform the task for which it has been designed. If this universal sufficiency is marred by its lack of universal efficacy, it is not universally sufficient and fails in its primary purpose.

Those who disagree with the teaching of our Reformers, often call themselves 'Moderate Calvinists'. Such a phrase reminds one of modern linguistic creations to deceive people into buying clothes. A garment made with synthetic fibres is advertised in terms of 'pure cashmere feeling' or a jacket is praised for its '100 per cent leather-look'. Such a new marketing term as 'Moderate Calvinism' was coined historically by those such as Alphonse Turretin, Richard Montague and New Divinity teachers influenced by Amyraldism and Neonomianism in their opposition to the orthodox, traditional Reformed teaching of the English Reformation. These 'Moderate Calvinists', in their zeal to eliminate the doctrines of grace from the Reformed agenda, are those who now call traditional and orthodox Calvinism 'Hyper-Calvinism', claiming that they alone are the true 'Calvinists' and stewards of common, saving grace. Thus, under the disguise of orthodox Calvinism, the Reformed faith is being dismantled doctrine by doctrine. The New Style Divinity offers a 'pure Calvinist feeling' or a 'Calvinist look' which is purely a synthetic imitation.

Looking for a Biblical and historical source for justification
To return to justification by faith, we find a steady re-awareness of the importance of the doctrine in the writings of our Reformers. They emphasised the practical aspect of justification centred in Christ's covenant from eternity to save them from their sins and the outworking of the Spirit in their lives. Though they realized that they stood pardoned and free of guilt before God solely through the imputed righteousness of Christ and not their own, they nevertheless believed that their freedom from condemnation was real and truly their own. They also believed that the faith given them was not merely an 'as if' recognition on the part of God but was a real lasting and transforming work in their souls. This conviction came gradually as our Reformers were freed from Rome's superstitions. The earliest Reformers who had spent a great part of their lives in Rome, had great difficulty in finding their theological legs and tidying up their theology in a thoroughly Reformed manner. We thus notice in Latimer's works how he grappled with the doctrines of election and predestination in relation to justification, seeing the connection more and more. By the time of the Elizabethan Settlement justification was widely seen as describing salvation in its entirety from God's decrees in eternity activated in time to man's glorification in his heavenly inheritance. This is why this writer prefers the works of these earlier Reformers and Puritans to their brethren of the following century as they had a more comprehensive understanding of the doctrines of grace as expressed in the gospel. As the hey-day of the Reformation and early Puritan period passed, we find a new, philosophical approach to the doctrine of salvation and a rationalistic interest in separating, analysing and systematising its inseparable parts. Theology, it appears, became amongst Protestants that which it had long been amongst papists – a branch of jurisprudence. Undoubtedly, it was Calvin's own legal training and analytical eye that prevented him from fully understanding the doctrines of grace taught by his

Justification

mentor Martin Bucer. Though Calvin relied on the bulk of Bucer's theology as his own, he could never come to terms with Bucer on justification. Thus a doctrinal legalism arose which strongly curbed the spontaneous spirituality and piety of the believer. Various check lists of doctrines were drawn up and used as criteria for church membership which led to new denominations separating from their brethren over their varied understanding of election, predestination, regeneration, conversion and sanctification, as if Christ, Paul and Apollos were divided. This love for separating the inseparable was applied also to church government and the inseparable Biblical doctrine of bishops and presbyters was challenged. It suddenly became more holy and a matter of personal salvation to be led by the one and not the other, so priestcraft, thrown out by our Reformers, once again reared its ugly head.

As the fire of the Reformation appeared to die out, such doctrinal lists of virtues, order and discipline were also used as a personal control on one's holiness. To test if one were in fellowship with Christ and fellow denominationalists, the serious Christian would find his assurance in ticking off those attributes of holiness on his list which he subjectively felt applicable to himself. This dividing of the indivisible caused by different ideas of holiness and sanctification gradually broke up the Reformation movement and invariably led to different ideas of justification. It is a clear fact of history that most of the errors and even heresies that crept into the Reformed movement did so due to an over-systematised and over-analysed scrutiny of doctrine. Blessings which belonged together such as election, the atonement, forgiveness of sins, justification and holiness were separated as if they had nothing at all to do with one another. Because only part views of such doctrines were attained through such studies, part understanding only ensued. Sadly William Perkins' works, especially *The Graine of Mustard-Seed* and *A Survey or Table, declaring the Order of the causes of Salvation and Damnation* were used as such check lists to holiness or 'law-books' in the New World, where religion gradually took on a regimented and law-bound face. These 'righteous overmuch' readers could spot a supposed triumph over sin in their lives and works of grace in their hearts by ticking off the points in Perkins' lists and then patting themselves on the back to congratulate themselves on their supposed growth in grace. In other words, they fell into the very trap against which Perkin's works warned. History has shown unmistakably that the troubles Governor Winthrop and John Cotton involved themselves in when dealing with their less legal but often more spiritual brothers and sisters in Christ was because they set up such check lists of holiness to produce their 'people of quality'. Such became new traditions of the elders and standards for citizenship, robbing the New World of the chance to ever become a Theocracy. This digression from the straight paths of Biblical righteousness paved the way for Jonathan Edwards' dichotomizing the sinner into his moral and natural abilities which New Divinity teaching embroidered into their legal duty-faith system which motivated a further departure from Reformed teaching on justification.

The doctrines of grace cannot be divided and isolated the one from the other. This is why earlier Reformed men referred to the doctrine of grace, i.e. in the singular. Towards the end of what we, perhaps mistakenly, call the 'Puritan Period', the term 'justification' had taken on a strictly forensic, legal, passive connotation, quite removed from the day to day challenges of the Christian life, growth in grace and holy living preached so fervently by our Reformers. Sadly, our modern Reformed theologians go less and less to the spring of the Reformation in their theology but derive their motives from the stale systematized 'Bodies of Doctrine' presented by later Precisians and Disciplinarians as a check list for personal holiness and means of controlling the work of the Spirit in individual sanctification. This has all sadly resulted in justification being seen as a mere legal declaration of pardon and a counter-reformation pathological interest in works righteousness as a sign that one is truly of the elect. This unnatural and un-Biblical preoccupation with one's own virtues is even put forward as the way to holiness by modern Reformed men who have lost those precious doctrines which go with justification such as the indwelling of the Holy Spirit and Christ within us who is our only hope of glory.[23]

---

[23] See Richard Alderson's *No Holiness, No Heaven!*, BOT, which is an exercise in pulling up one's own socks.

Justification

Chapter 2

The Reality and Finality of Justification

Biblical justification is both declarative and causative

Alan Cairns' *Dictionary of Theological Terms* is now in its third, expanded, edition and is thought to present the orthodox Reformed Faith as represented by the best of our modern Calvinists. Cairns defines justification as "the establishment of a sinner in a righteous standing before God" and tells us that the Biblical term behind the English, or rather Latin, word justification is dikaioo which means 'to declare or to demonstrate to be righteous'. Now to declare someone to be righteous can be a purely forensic declaration but to demonstrate that someone is righteous implies criteria other than legal. Righteousness must be found in a person so that one can demonstrate that it is in him. Cairns insists that God justifies the ungodly so he rules out rightly on Biblical grounds that any merit in men is effectual in justification. However, modern Reformed men query whether, indeed, a man has no faith before justification and whether he is transformed after justification. They see regenerating faith coming before justification and nothing after but the exhortation to repent and observe obedience to the law. They deny that the sinner is actually made just. These questions reveal the weakness of much modern teaching on justification. Modern Reformed expositors such as Leon Morris in his *Apostolic Preaching of the Cross*, see the term as having no causative meaning whatsoever, indeed no other meaning than being 'as if' one had been justified legally and fictitiously but not actually put in a state of justification. In other words, God can close His eyes to our unjust state but He cannot make us just. Thus Cairns states that our justification is merely forensic and does not really make us just. It does not change the sinner, it merely removes him from one legal

Justification

category 'condemnation' and places him in another legal category 'justification' with the idea behind it that the sinner is truly condemnable but not truly justifiable.

This is basically the view held by John Murray in his essay on justification in his *Systematic Theology*.[24] One might ask why I return time and time again to John Murray in my critical writings. My reason is that he has become the spokesman of that body of men who are radically emptying the general call of the gospel of our Reformed doctrines, albeit in the name of the Reformed faith. Murray says of justification that it is "an act of God, accomplished in time wherein God passes judgment with respect to us as individuals", and that "Justification is not the eternal decree of God with respect to us" thus denying that there is a once and for all eternity decree of God culminating in the once and for all time justifying sacrifice of the Son of God on behalf of the elect. This takes away the surety of salvation for the repentant sinner. When Murray decided to leave the Reformed gospel behind him by presenting his new divinity to the Fifteenth General Assembly of the Orthodox Presbyterian Church in 1948 alongside Arthur Kuschke and Ned Stonehouse, he caused a great rift in the Assembly. William Young and Floyd Hamilton protested in writing that Murray et. al. had not only no exegetical substantiation for their theory but their views were a clear contradiction of former Reformed teaching. Furthermore, Murray's colleagues told him that he would most certainly separate the Reformed churches from one another and split his denomination. The latter obvious deduction has sadly become the case. Today nothing causes rifts in the churches as much as Murray's profane idea that God desires what He is incapable of accomplishing and that our justification is not an irrevocable decision of God from eternity. Thus, keeping to his un-Reformed view of a merely legal justification, Murray goes on to argue:

> Justification is a judicial or forensic term and refers to a judgment conceived, recognized, and declared with respect to judicial status. It does not mean to make righteous or upright or holy in the subjectively factitive

---

[24] BOT, Vol. II, p. 202 ff. 1977.

and operative sense but to pronounce or declare to be righteous.[25]

Here Murray is, indeed, anxious to stress that justification is all of grace but he is equally anxious to stress that this grace is merely a legal grace, a contradiction in terms, bringing no blessings of grace to the one pronounced justified. The grounds of justification are accurately worked out by Murray but not the outworking of justification in the life of the believer. Murray stresses what God has done in the abstract, the symbolic and the theoretical but not what God does in us in concrete terms of practice, reality, re-creation and matter of fact. Murray thus answers the question what is the righteousness that justifies by abandoning Scripture and launching out nebulously and philosophically into flights of linguistic fancy and imaginative suppositions, declaring:

> When the righteousness contemplated in the constructive act is not ingenerated righteousness but an objective righteousness, the obedience of Christ wrought for us, this righteousness verifies and brings into clear light the pervasive forensic nature of justification even in that unique and distinctive ingredient that it is necessarily embraced in soteric justification. It verifies and vindicates the forensic character because it is putative in its nature, that is to say, that the element peculiar to soteric justification, namely, the constructive, is still strictly forensic in its nature. It is, in a word, the constituting of the judicial relation which is declared to be and it is such by the imputation to us of the righteousness and obedience of Christ.[26]

Fancy, when outlining the doctrine of justification in the gospel call to hungry souls waiting for saving justification, giving them such

---

[25] Ibid, p. 204.
[26] Ibid, pp. 214, 215.

a 'gospel'! This dark definition presents us with a dog chasing its tail. Murray is saying that justification is forensic because it is putative and because it is putative it is therefore forensic. If what Murray calls 'soteric justification' is merely another way of saying 'forensic justification is putative', then our justification is not real, nor is our faith and nor is our salvation. We are left with the 'gospel' that though Christ's righteousness is real, the justification which is wrought *for us* is not wrought *in us* and is merely a supposed justification, a legal fiction. How one misses the clear "Thus saith the Lord" of Scripture in Murray's bewildering pseudo-legal argumentation. Murray, however, says that he is not talking about legal fiction, he is talking about putative facts. But that which is putative is fiction until proved a fact. If I say that Tom is the putative father of Joe, it means that Tom is only said to be Joe's father. When God pronounces us just, we are truly justified and made joint heirs with Christ and accepted in Him, becoming truly His children. We are savingly justified and this saving justification is everything else but putative. Only because of this absolute reality have we peace with God (Romans 5:1). A putative justification can bring no peace but only anxiety as to whether it is true or not. Our sins are not only forgiven but our guilt is also removed and we are made new men in Christ Jesus. Our righteousness is imputed because it is Christ's righteousness which saves us, but our justifying salvation is not putative, it is real.

Biblical justification is a real and active gift of grace

Murray is thus totally woolly on what justification entails and when such justification is wrought out and granted. A justification which is received is not created on reception but is worked out by the judge beforehand who then declares the person free of guilt. Normally speaking, a court decision is only made when there are justifying grounds for it. All the court officials and jury may be long aware of the innocence of the defendant without the defendant knowing this. He has to wait until he receives the judge's verdict. Before that, however, there are many steps to be taken. All the steps in our Heavenly Judge's process of declaring a person justified and making him righteous are steps of mercy, a mercy promised and awarded to the elect before the dawn of time. The justified one, according to Ephesians, chapter 1, has already been blessed in Heaven having been placed in union with Christ and already been chosen before the foundation of the world to live a holy life. This blessed person has already been predestinated unto the adoption of children by Jesus Christ to Himself and the act of justification which Murray feels comes after the act of believing is merely God giving His elect what is theirs by divine choice from eternity and has been reserved for them until the time of grace destined for them.

Here Murray and his disciples in rejecting such Scriptural and Reformed truths are standing on radical, revolutionary ground indeed. Our Reformers, following Scripture, clearly taught that justification was a decree of God exercised in eternity and was part and parcel of God's decrees regarding election and predestination, faith not being separable from repentance, hope, love, good works etc..[27] Until recent times, Reformed ministers and scholars did not doubt this truth. Indeed, Louis Berkhof, writing in the BOT best-seller *Systematic Theology* under the title 'The Works of God', tells us that all God's works are decretal as He "worketh all things after the counsel of his will." When explaining the difficulties in relating God's decrees in eternity to time, Berkhof mentions especially creation and justification as such decrees.

Murray's doctrine is double-scepticism. He maintains that justification is not according to God's decretal will and also that even the desire in God for the justification of sinners is thwarted. Here, the Westminster Theological Seminary professor not only challenges the fact that the justification of individuals according to Scripture is the result of God's decrees but he also denies any connection between justification and the eternal nature and will of God for His people and views justification as a mere 'accomplishment in time'. This is, indeed, a new theology. Murray claims Buchanan's *Doctrine of Justification*,[28] as his authority for his negative views on justification. No such evidence is forthcoming in Buchanan. Though his theories of antitheses regarding justification do not always make it easy to

---

[27] See Bradford's *Defence of Election*, Parker Society, Vol. 1. Cranmer's, Bullinger's, Hooper's, Jewel's, Tyndale's and Nowell's works are full of this teaching. Indeed, is there a Reformer who does not accept this pan-Biblical teaching? It would appear not.
[28] BOT, pp. 251, 252.

understand his intention, Buchanan certainly comes nowhere near Murray's wayward teaching. Indeed, Buchanan obviously disagrees with the idea that there is no organic relationship between the purpose in God's mind and God's act in history and stresses that though justification takes place in the individual in time from man's point of view, it is solely as a result of God's purpose in eternity. Buchanan himself differs from the earlier Reformers here in their understanding of the relationship between God's purpose in eternity and His acts in time, seeing no parallelism in them. He has difficulty with the conception that God in eternity can also be immanent in His universe in time. It is as if Buchanan sees time as continuing *after* eternity. This is a common mistake in present Fullerite theology where eternity is invariably seen as 'past'.[29] Nevertheless, Buchanan places the will of God to justify the individual in eternity and he certainly does not believe erroneously as Murray that God's eternal desire to save all is thwarted by His own time, bound, yet decretal, will.[30] Murray would have difficulty indeed in finding a single Reformer to back him, here. Even Latimer, who often fought shy of referring to God's works in eternity, feeling it was perhaps too deep for his unevangelised hearers, nevertheless, when preaching on justification by faith, always took his hearers back to that phrase in Acts 13:48 "as many as were ordained to eternal life believed" and related this to divine election, predestination and justification.[31]

Justification as the finished work of Christ for us

Again, when claiming that justification is not "the finished work of Christ for us, when once-for-all he reconciled us to God by his death", Murray refers to Buchanan for support but again erroneously so. Buchanan in the passage referred to by Murray but not quoted

---

[29] See, for instance, Curt Daniel's booklet *Biblical Calvinism* in which he writes on page 5 of 'eternity past'. This reflects the problem such writers have with the relationship between eternity and time. They cannot envisage eternity impinging in time as it did at the crucifixion and resurrection of Christ and at justification. The idea of God activating his eternal decrees in time is foreign to them as they appear to believe that time is a period between two stages of eternity, one ending before time and one starting after time.

[30] See my New Focus article *Gospel of Deceit* for an analysis of Murray's god of two conflicting wills and his low view of the Trinity.

[31] See his sermons preached on 24th Jan., 1552; 7th and 14th Feb., 1552; Sermons and Remains of Hugh Latimer, *Works*, Vol. 2, Parker Society.

verbatim, stresses that justification means passing from death unto life and Christ is now 'our life', and there is no condemnation for those who are in Christ Jesus. He thus links atonement, justification and reconciliation. Buchanan gives Romans 5:2 amongst numerous other Scripture texts to support his argument. This must be read with verse 1 also in mind, "Therefore being justified by faith, we have peace with God through our Lord Jesus Christ: by whom also we have access by faith into his grace wherein we stand, and rejoice in hope of the glory of God." Here, in Scripture, we have a clear link between the finished work of Christ, justification and reconciliation. Matthew Henry's *Commentary* states explicitly that this is a reference to the saving work of Christ and reconciliation with God through Him and that 'justification and reconciliation are the first and primary fruit of the death of Christ'. Henry goes on to argue from Romans 9 and 10, that through the death of Christ we are justified by His blood and reconciled by His death. It would appear that Murray is striving to avoid the teachings that justification was either a decree of God's in eternity or the work of Christ in time. He sees it merely as the action of the sinner in coming to faith. However, as Murray believes that faith is a gift, he must also believe, if he is a Reformed man, that the justification which faith appropriates is also a gift and if it is a gift, it must have been God's to give before its reception by the ungodly. In other words, justification is a gift of saving grace but such grace does not come from nowhere but must have an origin. This is found according to our Reformers, who followed Scripture, in God's triune decreeing council whereby the elect were put in union with Christ in eternity when their justification was made sure and safe.

Justification

go *Topical*

Chapter 3

Justification Activates the Sinner to Lead a Righteous Life

The results of justification are outlined in the meaning of the term
Professor Murray does not face up to the practical question of what
happens to the sinner on being declared justified. Is he the same
ungodly person as before and has he still to follow the law to find
righteousness? Our Reformers did not waste time with such doubtful
disputations. In translating the term *dikaioo* and its many cognates,
they did not choose the term 'justify' arbitrarily. The components of
this word, from the Latin *justi* and *ficare*, truly mean 'to make just' or
'to make righteous'. Thus, when a Frenchman sees the word *justifier*,
or a German the term *rechtfertigen*, or as Luther preferred it,
rechtfertig machen, he can only think of being made just. Likewise,
dikaioo is rendered in Swedish *rättfärdiggörelse* (a making righteous)
and in Dutch *rechtvaardig maken* (to make righteous). Linguists will
note that in an effort to translate *dikaioo* and emphasise the causative
aspect exactly, Reformed translators into other tongues resorted to
tautology, reflecting Hebrew parallelism, stressing that God causes us
to be just and makes us righteous. English believers tend to forget
because of modern wayward teaching on justification, that the 'fy' in
'justify' means 'to make' as in the words 'deify', 'sanctify', 'clarify'
etc..

Dissenters from this view
This interpretation is challenged by those like Murray and Morris who
see a marked difference between the formal declaration of justification

Justification

in a legal sense and the fruits of justification through the indwelling of the Spirit in the person justified. Buchanan in his eighth lecture entitled *Justification: The Scriptural Meaning of the Term* queries whether one can use 'sanctify' and 'glorify' in a causative way as we speak of glorifying and sanctifying God which cannot be causative.[32] One can always use God as an exception as nobody and nothing is comparable with God, but when applied to God's actions concerning men, justifying, sanctifying and glorifying them, the meaning is strictly and, indeed, absolutely causative.

Dr R. C. Sproul in his essay on the forensic nature of justification in chapter 2 of the book *Justification by Faith Alone*[33] is obviously pulled both one way and another in dealing with the semantics of the verb 'to justify' and never appears to come to any settled conclusion. His linguistics, are, however, questionable. Going from the Hebrew *tsedaqah* (righteousness etc.) which he sees as the meaning behind the Greek *dikaiosun* (here, apparently *dikaiosunee* is meant) he concludes that 'to justify' is not a Biblical development of these terms but bears a meaning gained from 'Roman culture'. Now verbs are, we learn in the primary school, 'doing words' and thus their basic function is different to 'naming words' or nouns which have either a function as 'doers' or 'sufferers' of actions. It is therefore very risky linguistics to derive the activating nature of a verb in one language from nouns in other languages, which is the course Sproul takes. This risk is far greater when we actually have numerous cases of Hebrew and Greek verbs concerning justification used causatively. This Sproul appears to deny tacitly but he leaves the actual, expressed denial to Alister McGrath to whom he gives the last word on the alleged non-causative nature of 'to justify'. McGrath says:

> Augustine understands the verb justificare to mean 'to make righteous', an understanding of the term which he appears to have held throughout his working life … Although this is a permissible interpretation of the Latin

---

[32] *Doctrine of Justification*, pp. 226, 227.
[33] John MacArthur et al, Soli Deo Gloria, 1996.

word, it is unacceptable as an interpretation of the Hebrew concept which underlies it.[34]

This is a puzzling statement indeed from one who professes to be knowledgeable of the Biblical use of the Hebrew language. If we consider the verb *tzahdak* especially in its basic *Kal* (or *Qal*) forms it does often mean being merely in a state of righteousness without indicating that someone has been put into this state or made righteous by another. Yet Job's cry, "How then can man be justified?" (Job 40:8) certainly points to a desire in Job's heart to be made just, that is, made righteous. Indeed, such usage of the verb *tzahdak* is very common in the Old Testament as a brief glance in a Hebrew concordance will show. When we move from the *Kal* to the *Niphal* which is a passive form, we immediately find strongly causative action in the word, illustrated by Daniel 8:14 "then shall the sanctuary be cleansed". Moving on to what Weingreen calls the 'Intensive Active' moods such as *Piel, Pual, Hithpael* etc.,[35] we find many strongly causative usages of the verb in the Hebrew text such as the negative case of backsliding Israel attempting to justify herself (Jeremiah 3:11) and the positive case in Daniel 12:3 "And they that be wise shall shine as the brightness of the firmament; and they that turn many to righteousness as the stars for ever and ever." It must be difficult indeed to preach the call of the gospel if one is so bound up by linguistic misunderstanding that one thinks it wrong to preach the great truth that justification is God's act in turning sinners to righteousness. Happily, Paul, a Hebrew of the Hebrews, freely preached "For as one man's disobedience many were made sinners, so by the obedience of one shall many be made righteousness" (Romans 5:19). Our preaching is based on the gospel fact that in justifying sinful men, God makes them new creatures.

The uncertain voice with which the various contributors to the book *Justification Alone* speak is obviously caused by the false antithesis they set up to warn their readers rightly against the Roman idea of initial justification at baptism and the earning of subsequent

---

[34] Ibid, p. 28. The quote is taken from McGrath's *Justia Dei*, Vol. I, pp. 30, 31.
[35] *A Practical Grammar for Classical Hebrew*, Oxford, 1959, p. 100.

Justification

inherent righteousness. The authors tell us that there is either a justification which is purely declarative and forensic or we must believe that the sinner is able to work out his own justification. R. C. Sproul puts his dilemma, which he does not really try to solve, in the following words,

> In simple terms the issue boils down to this: Are we justified by a process by which we become actually just or are we justified by a declarative act by which we are counted or reckoned to be just by God? Are we declared just or are we made just by justification?[36]

An acceptable, Biblical way out of Dr Sproul's dilemma is to point out that his antithesis is artificial. The correct Biblical choice the Bible presents is either to believe that God makes His justified ones fit for heaven or believe that the sinner can make himself fit. It is foreign to the Biblical definitions of God's justifying work in Christ through the Spirit to believe that justification is a mere title-deed to a freedom from punishment with no justifying work done in the holder of that deed. Indeed, the logical consequence of such a belief would be to act as the papists do and look for an alternative way of being justified both in name and nature. Justification entails making just men perfect. It gives them a love for the righteous ways of their Saviour. This is not separate from the work of justification but an integral part of that work. Without this integral part of justification, there would be no sanctification and no holiness. Holiness is being of that mind which is in Christ Jesus. There is no perfecting work of Christ and the Spirit in the believer unless that person is accounted justified to that end. The decretal, the declarative and the glorifying aspect are all one and the activation of them all eternal. A person can never be more justified than when God decrees to give him faith and imputes Christ's righteousness to him. Nor can he ever be more justified than when Christ is working His purpose out in him. From the moment of justification, he is safe for all eternity in the hands of Jesus. Sadly, as we see from the testimony of those who view justification as 'strictly'

---

[36] Op. cit. p. 25.

or 'merely' forensic, that after justification, we are invariably taught to cleave to the so-called moral law and find our practical holiness through that instrument. Returning to Sinai never made a justified soul holy but has made hypocrites and Pharisees of many.

Justification is putting the elect where they belong
If we examine the Hebrew, Pali and Sandskrit equivalents of *dikaioo* (*tzad, dik, dhammika, dharmya* etc. and cognates) we find the term referring not only to a legal pronouncement as 'lawful' or 'just' but being in an actual state of lawfulness or justness. If we go back to our most ancient Indo-European languages in New Testament times and beyond, we find the word for 'just' meaning 'placed on a solid foundation or throne'. Thus in keeping with this ancient meaning, the Scriptures tell us that in justification we are granted the privilege of sitting with Christ on His throne and of reigning with Him (1 Corinthians 3:11; Revelation 3:21). Both Semitic and Indo-European sources describe the root meaning of the term 'justify' as 'to be put where one belongs'. Thus, in being justified, we are placed in the Beloved, where we have belonged from eternity. Surely such a status far transcends the mere forensic and gives full glory to God for the way He has changed us. Ephesians 1:6 tells us the wonderful news of the gospel whereby we were placed in Christ before the foundation of the world and made acceptable in the Beloved. One cannot be more 'causative' than that! Nor can one be too comprehensive in expressing the practical and activating blessings with which God endues His elect.

It is thus no surprise to find that our Greek lexica tell us that *dikaioo* and its cognates means in its active and passive forms, to declare just, to vindicate, to verify, to cleanse, to do justice to, to make just, to make good, to make free, to make pure, to become pure, to set free, to be freed from sin, to prove God right – all through participation in Christ's righteousness imputed to the believer. No matter what NT Greek lexicon of note we pick up,[37] we will find abundant Biblical passages quoted in them to illustrate this usage. Hermann Cremer alone in his *Biblisch-Theologisches Wörterbuch*

---

[37] In preparation, I have used Bauer, Liddell and Scott, Thayer, Hatch/Redpath, Muller, Gemoll, Wigram and Cremer.

Justification

devotes 36 pages of small type to the manifold meanings of *dikaoo's* cognates and Hebrew counterparts related to the Scriptural doctrine of justification. Sadly, as in the baptism debate, writers often take one meaning out of many from popular, secular dictionaries to interpret the multifarious Bible teaching. So too, those who are offended by the Biblical doctrine of justification, would rather trust in one single secular meaning of the term which they can bend their way for their righteousness rather than dig deep into the semantic and theological cornucopias of the Scriptures.

Justified sinners are changed sinners

The righteousness given to us by grace, through the faith of the Lord Jesus Christ, however, is not a sham or make-believe but a real partaking of the divine nature. It is a justifying righteousness which cleanses from all sin, pardons and removes every guilty stain and transforms men. Such justified ones are thus called in Scripture *New Creatures* and the *Born Again*. They can say, "I am crucified with Christ: nevertheless I live; yet not I, but Christ liveth in me: and the life which I now live in the flesh I live by the faith of the Son of God, who loved me and gave himself for me." This transforming, undeserved, justifying work in the elect is well illustrated by Christ's parable in Luke 18:9, 14 culminating in the words:

> And the publican, standing afar off, would not lift up so much as his eyes unto heaven, but smote upon his breast, saying, God be merciful to me a sinner. I tell you, this man went down to his house justified rather than the other: for every one that exalteth himself shall be abased; and he that humbleth himself shall be exalted.

Here, it is obvious that the publican had become a changed man through his justification. Surely, to ask the question "Who made him just?" is legitimate here and the only answer can be "God". Thus the elect sinner is called out of this world to be a *New Man* in Christ Jesus, "created in righteousness and holiness," (Ephesians 4:24; Colossians 3:10) called "to the general assembly and church of the firstborn, which are written in heaven, and to God the judge of all, and to the spirits of just men made perfect," (Hebrews 13:23).

After meditating somewhat on the enormous scope of the doctrine of justification, it will be profitable to see how our Reformers and the Puritans viewed the subject in their pastoral and evangelistic work.

Justification

Part Two
The Teaching of the English Reformers and Early Puritans

Chapter 1

Sixteenth Century Reformers

William Tyndale (c. 1494-1536)

William Tyndale, at the beginning of the Reformation, believed that the doctrine of justification was the key to a correct understanding of the whole of Scripture and everything appertaining to Christ's salvation. Tyndale emphasised that justification was entirely at God's initiative, given to the elect before ever a man was born or had sinned. In *The Parable of the Wicked Mammon*[38] and *Answer to St Thomas More*[39] Tyndale explains that God never justifies a man passively but actively with a works-producing faith. Whilst he is justified by God through faith promised to the elect, he is justified before men by his works. Justification, Tyndale teaches, is the same as forgiveness of sins. When the Father has brought the sinner to despair of himself before the law and presents the Son to him in His passion and death, He says:

> This is my dear Son, and He hath prayed for thee, and hath suffered all this for thee; and for his sake I will forgive thee all that thou has done against this good law,

---

[38] Tyndale's *Works*, Vol. 1, Parker Society, especially p. 48 ff.
[39] See especially chapter 11, Book Four, Vol. 3, Parker Society, pp. 193, 210.

Justification

and I will heal thy flesh and teach thee to keep this law, if thou learn. And I will bear with thee, and take all a worth that thou doest, till thou canst do better; and in the main season, notwithstanding thy weakness, I will yet love thee no less than I do the angels in heaven so that thou wilt be diligent to learn. And I will assist thee, and keep thee and defend thee, and be thy shield and care for thee. And the heart here beginneth to mollify and wax soft, and to receive health, and believeth the mercy of God, and in believing is saved from the fear of everlasting death, and made sure of everlasting life; and then, being overcome with this kindness, beginneth to love again and to submit herself unto the laws of God, to learn them and to walk in them."[40]

Tyndale argues that first God appoints mercy and grace to the elect whom He has chosen, then He sends the Spirit to open their eyes and give them faith which, in turn, gives them peace with God and causes them to understand their justification. Thus justification always goes before regeneration and faith. Just as man is condemned in eternity before he ever sinned in his person, so the elect are chosen and justified in eternity before they ever came to faith. Faith is God's gift to those He justifies and the elects' means of appropriating justification. Faith receives the mercy whereby God justifies us and forgives us. Faith testifies to our heart that we are justified and its deeds justify us outwardly and externally before men, showing that we are justified inwardly before God. Concerning repentance, Tyndale emphasises that it is not my repentance that procures my justification but "a light that the Spirit of God hath given me, out of which light repentance springeth."[41] Tyndale can write like this because he believes that the security of the elect in Christ goes back beyond the beginning of time and he can thus say in the Prologue to the Book of Exodus, "The New Testament was ever, even from the beginning of the world" and it was at this first awakening of creation that the

---

[40] Ibid, p. 194.
[41] Ibid, p. 196.

justifying promises of Christ went out to His elect. The justifying work of God in Christ is found in the timelessness of eternity.[42] All the blessings which an elect soul has in Christ are reserved in heaven for him, revealed to him in time and glorify him in eternity. This is gospel preaching and without this emphasis on God's saving work in eternity our modern Reformed churches, call them what they may, are not Reformed and do not preach justification by faith.

John Bradford (1510-1555)

John Bradford, the Protestant martyr, firmly anchors justification in the elective decrees of God saying in his Defence of Election: "God hath of his own mercy and good will, and to the 'praise of his glory' in Christ, elected some, and not all; whom he hath predestined unto everlasting life in the same Christ, and in his time 'calleth them, justifies them and glorifieth them', so that 'they shall never perish' and err to damnation finally."[43]

Bradford explains how the calling to justification is the predestination of it and election to it and continues: "whereby we see that predestination nor election is not universal to all, for all be not justified."[44] Elsewhere, Bradford says he 'wades in predestination'[45] and that regenerating and justifying faith is a gift from God to those whom God 'before the beginning of the world, hath predestinated, in Christ unto eternal life.'[46] Bradford refused to separate justification from the forgiveness of sins, regeneration and sanctification.[47] Bradford states that justification:

> ... precedeth regeneration, from whom we may discern it, but not divide it, no more than heat from fire. Justification in scripture is taken for the forgiveness of our sins, and consisteth in the forgiveness of our sins.

---

[42] Tyndale, Vol. 1, p. 417. See also in Vol. 1, *The Manner and Order of Our Election*, pp. 35 ff.. It would reward the reader's industry to look up the numerous entries for justification, faith and election in Tyndale's works so as to obtain an overall picture.

[43] *Works*, Vol. I, p. 311.

[44] *Works*, Vol. I, p. 314.

[45] Miles Coverdale's *Godly Letters of the Martyrs*, London, 1837, p. 314 ff.

[46] Ibid, p. 315.

[47] See John Murray, *Works*, Vol. 2, 17, Justification, where Murray separates justification from these graces.

Justification

> This is only God's work, and we nothing else but patients (receivers) and not agents. After this work, in respect of us and our sense, cometh regeneration, which altogether is God's work also: for, as to our first birth we bring nothing, so we bring nothing that can help to our justification; as St Austin full well said, 'He that made thee without thee, shall he not justify thee without thee?'
>
> Good men ... are content to give no less to God justifying and regenerating them, than they do to their parents for their first generation. Afore we be justified and regenerated of God, we are altogether dead to God and to all goodness in his sight; and therefore we are altogether patients till God hath wrought this his only work, justification and regeneration. Which work, in respect of us and our imperfection and falls, in that it is not so full and perfect that it may be more and more, therefore by the Spirit of sanctification (which we receive in regeneration as the seed of God) we are quickened to labour with the Lord, and to be more justified; that is, by faith and the fruits of faith, to ourselves and to others to declare the same; and so to increase from virtue to virtue, from glory to glory, having always need to have our feet washed, although we be clean notwithstanding."[48]

Justification, for Bradford, is God's act in eternity whereby he elected His chosen ones to salvation. Thus justification is inseparable from regeneration, the new birth, the forgiveness of sins or any other act of God in Christ in redemption. Nor can justification in eternity be separated from God's working out this justification in our lives in time. Therefore, with justification comes sanctification so that we may grow in grace and the knowledge of our Saviour. This enables us to be justified, as Bradford says 'to ourselves and to others'. We are 'clean notwithstanding' because our sins have been washed clean away and we stand righteous before God. But we are not righteous before others until they see Christ's justifying faith in us and a work of the Spirit.

---

[48] From A Treatise of Election and Free Will, *Works*, Vol. 1, pp. 217, 218.

Thomas Becon (c. 1512-1567)

This most neglected Reformer outlines his doctrine of justification in *The Common Places of the Holy Scripture*, stating that though faith works by charity, works of faith have nothing to do with justification and any belief that justification is through faith and works "obscureth not only the dignity of faith, but also the price of redemption, which was brought to pass by the blood of Christ."[49] He tells those who look for justification through sincere obedience, that "if righteousness come of the law, then Christ is dead in vain" (Galatians 3:10, 11). Faith is the fulfilment of the promises of God, "It is the gift of God, and cometh not of works, lest any man should boast." Becon argues that justification is far from being merely legal in its effect and application but rather:

> A Christian man that is justified by faith is compared in the holy scripture to 'a tree planted by the river-side, which bringeth forth his fruit in due season'. As the sun cannot be without light, nor the fire without heat; no more can the true and the Christian faith be without good works, whensoever occasion is offered either for the glory of God or for the profit of our neighbour. If faith ceaseth to work, then it is not an evangelical, but an historical faith; yea, then it is that faith whereof St. James speaketh, saying: 'As the body without the spirit is dead; so likewise is faith without works dead.' For, as the apostle saith: 'We are the workmanship of God, created in Christ Jesu unto good works, which God hath prepared that we should walk in them.'[50]

Becon ends this work with a summary of his doctrines with proof-texts. Of free-will, he says, "Free-will, without the grace of God, can do nothing in matters of faith and everlasting salvation," quoting thirty Scripture passages as proof. He introduces justification as the divine

---

[49] Vol. III, p. 291.
[50] Ibid, p. 291.

Justification

alternative to free-will, saying, "That so many as are justified and saved are justified and saved only by the alone and free mercy of God through faith." This is backed up by thirty-one Scripture texts. Becon sees duty-faith teaching as a Roman dogma and contradicts it by declaring that there are no justifying rewards gained by courting favour with God through duties. This would be working for righteousness. The Bible says:

> ... to him that worketh not, but believeth on him that justifieth the ungodly, is his faith counted for righteousness. Even as David describeth the blessedness of that man unto whom God imputeth righteousness without deeds: Blessed are they whose unrighteousness are forgiven, and whose sins are covered. Blessed is that man to whom the Lord will not impute sin.[51]

Becon taught that not only was the faith which the justified received implanted in him by God but also the good works which were the fruit of justification. In his *Demands of Holy Scripture*, Becon outlines all the doctrines of grace. On coming to predestination, he says that the elect were "predestinate by the grace of God to this vocation, election, justification and salvation, before the beginning of the world." On justification, he says, "What is justification? Of unrighteous to be made righteous by the righteousness of Christ, which we conceive by faith."[52]

In his *Common Places*, Becon teaches "Christ is the fulfilling of the law, to justify all that believe." God has freed His people from the law by justifying them by grace. People freed by God are not put under a further legal yoke.[53] Becon's view of justification is at once practical, empirical and future-orientated. He rejects the teaching that God in Christ has done nothing for His elect in justification other than legally freeing them.

---

[51] Ibid, pp. 328, 331.
[52] Ibid, p. 616.
[53] Ibid, pp. 339, 340.

Alexander Nowell (c. 1507-1602)

Nowell's Catechism, which clearly maintains the Reformed doctrine of justification, was put forward by the Church of England as their definitive catechism for doctrinal instruction. Nowell argues that Christ is our justification from eternity and uses the terms 'God's mercy' and 'God's decrees' interchangeably as synonyms. He argues that, "all those whom God hath chosen he hath restored unto holiness of life and innocency."[54] Nowell, the master, asks the scholar he has brought to faith, "Doth not then our own godliness toward God, and leading of our life honestly and holily among men, justify us before God?" The scholar answers:

> S: If any man were able to live uprightly according to the precise rule of the law of God, he should worthily be counted justified by his good works. But seeing we are all most far from that perfection of life, yea, and be so oppressed with conscience of our sins, we must take another course, and find another way, how God may receive us into favour, than by our own deservings.
>
> M: What way?
>
> S: We must flee to the mercy of God, whereby he freely embraces us with love and good will in Christ, without any of our deserving, or respect of works, both forgiving us our sins, and so giving us the righteousness of Christ by faith in him, that for the same Christ's righteousness he so accepted us, as if it were our own. To God's mercy therefore through Christ we ought to impute all our justification.
>
> M: How do we know it to be thus?
>
> S: By the gospel, which containeth the promises of God by Christ, 'to the which when we adjoin faith, that is to say, an assured persuasion of mind and steadfast confidence of God's good-will, such as hath been set out in the whole Creed, we do, as it were, take state and possession of this justification that I speak of.

---

[54] *Nowell's Catechism*, 1570, Parker Society reprint, p. 172.

Justification

M: Dost not thou then say that faith is the principal cause of this justification, so as by the merit of faith we are counted righteous before God?

S: No; for that were to set faith in the place of Christ. But the spring-head of this justification is the mercy of God, which is conveyed to us by Christ, and is offered to us by the gospel, and received of us by faith as with a hand.

M: Thou sayest then that faith is not the cause but the instrument of justification; for that it embraceth Christ, which is our justification; coupling us with so strait bond to him, that it maketh us partakers of all his good things?

S: Yea forsooth.

M: But can this justification be so severed from good works, that he that hath it can want them?

S: No: for by faith we receive Christ such as he delivereth himself unto us. But he doth not only set us at liberty from sins and death, and make us at one with God, but also with the divine inspiration and virtue of the Holy Ghost doth regenerate and newly form us to the endeavour of innocency and holiness, which we call newness of life.

M: Thou sayest then that justice, faith, and good works, do naturally cleave together, and therefore ought no more to be severed, than Christ, the author of them in us, can be severed from himself.

S: It is true.

M: Then this doctrine of faith doth not withdraw men's minds from godly works and duties?

S: Nothing less. For good works do stand upon faith as upon their root. So far, therefore, is faith from withdrawing our hearts from living uprightly, that, contrariwise, it doth most vehemently stir us up to the endeavour of good life; yea and so far, that he is not truly faithful that doth not also to his power both shun vices and embrace virtues, so living always as one that looketh to give an account. [55]

---

[55] Ibid, pp. 180, 181.

go *Topical*

Nowell emphasises the practical joys the redeemed have in contemplating their justification. They know that Christ appeases the wrath of His Father and thus their sins will never be imputed to them again and that they are beloved of God.[56] Their lives are now in God's care and He reveals His justification to them in justice, faith and good works.

Thomas Rogers (c.1523-1615)
Thomas Rogers on the Thirty-Nine Articles[57] is all gold. In his remarks on Articles Eleven and Seventeen, he teaches a. that that predestination and election is to eternal life; b. 'Predestination hath been from everlasting'; c. none of the predestinated can perish; d. only certain men are predestinated to such life; God's will and purpose alone determines who is elected and who is not; e. all the elect are called both outwardly by the Word and inwardly by the Holy Spirit; f. by predestination in eternity, justification is given the elect, as also the faith of Christ and sanctification of the Spirit and glorification in the life to come and g. these doctrines are most comfortable to the godly wise but deadly dangerous for carnal people. Rogers' explains that this justification is not by the works of the law but by the faith of Jesus Christ (Galatians 2:16) which was determined and sealed before the foundation of the world (Ephesians 1:4) and all the blessings of salvation were given to the elect in Christ before the world was (2 Timothy 1:9). Rogers condemns as adversaries to the truth, those who would see God 'included within the compass of any time' in his electing, predestinating and justifying work and not in eternity. Rogers thus affirms, "He hath chosen us in Christ &c., and hath predestinated us through Christ unto himself Ephesians 1:4, 5. Ye were not redeemed with corruptible things &c., but with the precious blood of Christ, as of a Lamb undefiled and without spot, which was ordained before the foundation of the world, but was declared in the last times for your sakes (1 Peter 1:18, 20). The purposes of God always remain according to election (Romans 9:11)."

---

[56] Ibid, p. 143.
[57] Part One published in 1579 and Part Two in 1586.

Justification

Chapter 2

Seventeenth Century Puritans

Thomas Goodwin (1600-1680)
This theological but controversial giant, called 'Patriarch and Atlas of Independency' left England in the days of Laud's High Church dictatorship to assist John Archer with his English merchant congregation at Arnheim in Holland. After taking part in several church quarrels in Arnheim and Rotterdam, Goodwin returned to England at the beginning of the Great Rebellion and represented Independency at the Westminster Conference. There he joined a handful of dissenters who protested at the intolerance of the Presbyterian majority but was unsuccessful and so appealed to Parliament with a measure of success. This endeared him to Cromwell. The Independents, however, found themselves forced to retire from the Assembly. When the political tide turned against the Presbyterians under Cromwell's preference for Congregationalism, Goodwin received many honours including the presidency of Magdalen College, Oxford. At the Restoration under Charles II, Goodwin was deprived of his university post but allowed to set up a Congregational church in Fetter Lane, London. Goodwin's major work *Justifying Faith* was first published posthumously with his collected works in 1681-1704. It was last reprinted from the 1863 Nichol edition in 1985 by the Banner of Truth Trust. Goodwin became the standard Puritan author on justification by faith until his work was

Justification

rivalled but certainly not bettered by James Buchanan's *The Doctrine of Justification* in 1867.

In his *Justifying Faith*, Goodwin takes into account the new wayward, rationalist teaching on common grace which was being displayed as a stepping stone to faith rewarded by justification, thus again, as in pagan papist times, striving to equate faith with reason and natural law. In refuting this teaching, Goodwin argued that there was no 'door of faith' to be found in nature because that door is 'utterly shut up' as a pointer to God's mercies. These are only revealed in Christ and it is only in Christ that faith can be received and recognized as a token of justifying grace. Goodwin uses the story of Noah to show that nature is not a stepping stone to faith, indeed, it does not present us with "the smallest twig for a positive act of faith to set foot upon".[58] Referring to the merciful aspects of God's nature seen by Moses in Exodus 34, Goodwin teaches that nature can assist faith when once it is there but can in no way point to, let alone lead to, faith.[59]

In Book I, Chapter VI, Goodwin outlines how God determined in eternity to chose a people for Himself and give them the power to be His children making them what they were not. He then explains:

> It is thus also in justification. It is calling us from what we are not, yea, from the contrary, to be righteous in his righteousness, by the power and dominance of him that is Jehovah, the fountain of being, who says to an ungodly person, 'Thou art righteous' and in saying it makes him such: Romans 5:19.

This is what Goodwin calls the 'forensic act of pronouncing a man innocent at the bar'. But Goodwin does not stop here. Under the same heading of justification, he continues:

> God comes to a soul that is nothing but sin, and gives it a new heart, and a new spirit, and it becomes a work-

---

[58] Op. cit., Book I, Chapter II, pp. 8, 9.
[59] Op. cit., Book I, Chapter V, p. 19 ff..

manship created to good works, this he does by working this new creature in it, by internal changing our corrupt hearts, as one day he will do our vile bodies.

Thus, for Goodwin, a keen analyst, there are two characteristics of justification, justification from eternity and justification in Christ. This he sees as the declaring to be justified and the re-creation of the justified one when he is put in Christ. He outlines that faith is the grace given to man to appropriate the justification given and accept the changes God makes in him. He explains in Book I, Chapter XV, that the person to be justified is decreed as such in eternity according to God's covenant transactions with His Son. Thereupon, this person is always counted justified by God. However, this justification from eternity consists in the elect sinner being represented before God by Christ. That is, the sinner's justification does not yet exist in himself but only in his covenant union with Christ until the sinner has a being and is granted faith. In other words, the elect sinner needs to receive justifying faith in time. So Goodwin believed in a justification from eternity seen from God's point of view and a justification in time from man's point of view. He, however, taught justification in three stages or rather dimensions rather than two. Christ undertook in eternity by covenant with the Father to remove all the sins and debts from the people given to Him by the Father. By means of this covenant, the Father discharged all elect sinners from their sentence of guilt and justified them by stipulation. In the fullness of time Christ atoned for the sins of the elect and God justified His Son and with Him the elect. This vicarious act resulted in a justification by representation. When Christ finally knits the elect sinner to Himself by the Spirit and works faith in him, then God pronounces him righteous in himself because of Christ's righteousness imputed to him. This is justification by personal application. According to Goodwin, there is no personal justification without faith but faith is applied to the justified, one as a sign and seal of justification but not as its prior cause. John Gill, whose view of justification was discussed in my *John Gill And Justification From Eternity*, was greatly influenced by Goodwin, Witsius, Ames, Rutherford, Twisse, Macovius, Pemble, and Hoornbeeck, all of whom

Justification

held to the Reformed doctrine of Justification from eternity applied to the sinner in from three (Goodwin) to seven (Witsius) stages. Gill extended Goodwin's three stages to cover eternity and what Gill called aeviternity, a term which describes the life span of the Christian from birth, through the new birth and physical death up to and including the period of the believer's eternal inheritance in Heaven when time shall be no more. Thus Gill's three stages refer to justification *in foro Dei*, that is as an eternal, immanent act of God's; *in foro conscientiae*, which is a declarative act to and upon the conscience of the believer; and *in foro mundi* which is an act of God's that will be declared to men and angels in the last judgment leading to the elect sinner's glorification.[60] These stages are very similar to those taught by Martin Bucer.[61]

Goodwin was often very complicated and occasionally ambiguous and diffusive in his discussions concerning justification as he sought to view the doctrine both from God's action and man's response, especially as he spoke of man exercising faith by his 'own consent'.[62] He lived at a time when the plain and simple teaching of the Reformation period was having to give way to political theology. His main teaching, however, on justification was quite clear, stressing that no man had the will to consent unless given him by God who is "the forger of every link of that golden chain".[63] Yet, it is perhaps thus no wonder that as the emphasis on God's sovereignty in justification began to be challenged in the coming generations, the more man-centred followers of the new divinity mentioned by Traill below snapped up any 'evidence' they could find to 'prove' that they were in the tradition of the Puritans in stressing human consent in justification. In Goodwin, we see the development of analytical theology which gave theological dissent more than a twig to perch on in their efforts to see salvation from man's point of view rather than God's.

---

[60] *Sermons and Tracts*, pp. 459, 460.
[61] See Philip Eveson's excellent essays on Bucer in Issues 457, 458 of the BOT magazine. Bucer's teaching on justification is discussed in Issue 458. As so often in Banner articles, doctrines are praised in characters they find positive whereas the same doctrines are condemned in other saints whom they consider 'Antinomians'. Actually, Bucer was far more a High Calvinist on a number of issues than Gill. A fact which does not take away his value in the least.
[62] Book I, Chapter XV, p. 139.
[63] Book I, Chapter VI., p. 39.

John Bunyan (1628-1688)

Few Christian readers will be unaware of the brave life and testimony of this spiritual giant who spent so many years persecuted by a Restitution Church and Government who seemed to place all their fury due to their own sufferings under Cromwell's regime on the innocent head of this scapegoat, a poor but brilliant tinker from Bedford. Though called the 'Immortal Dreamer' by his spiritual successors for his great literary masterpiece *Pilgrim's Progress*, Bunyan was no visionary theorist but a man of flesh and blood who preached to men of flesh and blood and led them on to a practical religion seldom attained to in the history of the English Church. Though Bunyan's testimony has reaped the acclamation of all good men throughout the world for 350 years, Bunyan often stood alone with his troubles but for God, persecuted not only by his Latitudinarian enemies in the Church of England such as Edward Fowler and the barbarous laws which supported them but scorned and defamed also by the sacramental Pharisees of the Baptist churches such as Fifth Monarchy man Colonel D'Anvers and William Kiffin. These let their baptismal waters wash away their brethren in the faith and become "the rule, the door, the bolt, the bar, the wall of division between the righteous and the unrighteous" and despised Bunyan for his humble birth.[64] Bunyan was no denominationalist and thus sadly criticised by most denominationalist bigots who put their church externals before Christian fellowship.

Bunyan's work on justification entitled *A Defence of the Doctrine of Justification*,[65] printed during his lifetime, was written, like so many of his great works, in prison. The occasion was the publication of a book entitled *The Design of Christianity* written by Edward Fowler the rector of Northill, Bedford, later Bishop of Gloucester. Bunyan's honest position as a Dissenter was that Fowler's work was alien to the Thirty-Nine Articles and thus to the saving gospel. In this work, Fowler stresses the importance of the 'natural' or 'moral' law as a natural path to righteousness and which is not only recognizable by

---

[64] See T. Paul's and W. Kiffin's *Some serious reflections on that part of Mr. Bunyan's Confession of faith, touching church communion with unbaptised believers* and Bunyan's reply, *Differences in judgment about water baptism, no bar to communion.*

[65] Offor, Vol. II, p. 278 ff.

Justification

the right reason of every man but can also be followed by man leading to a positive development in personal holiness. He teaches that man's true destiny is to undo all the sins made by Adam and thus regain that righteousness which Adam enjoyed before the fall. Bunyan who is mostly silver, if not golden tongued in his other works, becomes at times most scathing in his reply to Fowler, recognising full well that Fowler's doctrines taught a Christianity without Christ or any kind of atonement for sin. Indeed, the Anglican who was so negligent of his own Articles taught that revealed religion was very much secondary to natural law. Modern readers will find much of Fowler in the emphasis on 'the nature and fitness of things' in Latitudinarianism, Grotianism, the New Divinity and Fullerism.

Bunyan points out that the righteousness of the law can only end in leading man from the only true righteousness which is the righteousness of Christ imputed to man by grace. The law is there to point a finger of accusation at man but grace is there to pronounce him free from guilt and justify him savingly. Christians, in keeping with Paul in Philippians 3:7, 9 do not look for any deserving righteousness of their own because they know they have none but they seek union with Christ in whom they find a perfect righteousness, the righteousness which is of God by faith. Bunyan tells Fowler straight that all human righteousness is 'dogs meat' and no use to anyone in matters of justification and salvation. Indeed, Bunyan denies that any righteousness at all is to be obtained by following the so-called moral law, either before or after coming to an awareness of faith. True justifying righteousness is laid in the believer by the Holy Ghost Himself. This gives the believer a superior righteousness to that of Adam and demonstrates to us that any dependence on Adamic righteousness can only lead to Adamic failure. Justification is, put simply, "If any man have not the Spirit of Christ, he is none of his (Romans 8:9). The justified soul is given holy principles such as love, joy and peace, all of which are not natural but spiritual. Thus our holy actions are entirely due to spiritual gifts given us and not natural gifts with which we are naturally born. The consequence is that being made free from our natural bondage to sin by the faith of Christ alone, "we have our fruit unto holiness, and the end everlasting life" (Romans 6:22). The very root of Christianity, Bunyan argues, is not any design of man but predestination, calling, adoption and justification by Christ's blood, while we in ourselves are sinners. He sums up this section on what makes a man righteous by stating that three things are essential to inward gospel holiness, 1. The Holy Ghost, 2. Faith in Christ, 3. A new heart, and a new spirit. It is to be noted here that there is no talk in Bunyan about a justification separated from holiness, nor of an active justification and a passive justification, nor a forensic justification and a justification of sincere obedience but one practical justification which entails God's righteous lifting of the sentence of guilt and punishment and His righteous fruits in the elect believer. Bunyan explains to Fowler that the Spirit is not received through doing the works of the law but by the hearing of faith (Galatians 3:2). Though the righteousness of the law can only condemn us, the righteousness of faith in the Lord Jesus Christ, wrought out and provided by Him, justifies us and delivers us from the curse of that very law which such as Fowler serve. The promise of justification is not made to those who follow the law "for the law is not of faith; therefore they only that are of faith are blessed with faithful Abraham."[66]

Fowler maintained that Christ did not procure any absolute blessings for His people but merely promised blessings on condition of belief. Bunyan answers:

> By the death of Christ was the forgiveness of sins effectually obtained for all that shall be saved, and they, even while yet enemies, by that were reconciled unto God. So that, as to forgiveness from God, it is purely upon the account of grace in Christ (Romans 5:9, 10; Colossians 1:20; Ephesians 4:32). So then, our effectual believing is not a procuring cause in the sight of God, or a condition of ours foreseen by God, and the motive that prevailed with him to forgive us our manifold transgressions: Believing being rather that which makes application of that forgiveness, and that possesseth the soul with that peace that already is made for us with God, by the blood of his Son Christ Jesus (Romans 5:1). The

---

[66] Ibid, p. 290.

61

peace and comfort of it cometh not to the soul, but by believing. Yet the work is finished, pardon procured, justice being satisfied already, or before, by the precious blood of Christ.

Observe, I am commanded to believe, but what should I believe? Or what should be the object of my faith in the matter of my justification with God? Why, I am to believe in Christ, I am to have faith in his blood? But what is it to believe in Christ? And what to have faith in his blood? To believe that while we were yet sinners Christ died for us, that even then, when we were enemies, we were reconciled to God by the death of his Son: To believe that there is a righteousness *already* (Bunyan's emphasis) for us completed.[67]

Thus Bunyan can sum up by saying that Christ puts His elect in a personal possession of justifying pardon "before we know it".

Bunyan develops his doctrine of imputed righteousness briefly in the above mentioned work and in his *A Confession of My Faith*.[68] His major work on the subject *Justification By an Imputed Righteousness Or No Way to Heaven but by Jesus Christ*[69] was not discovered amongst his papers until after his death. Though Bunyan's usual preface is missing and a few parts are obviously unfinished, the work is a masterly defence of the Biblical doctrine over which many a modern so-called Reformed man stumbles. In this great work, Bunyan wishes to show that, "There is no way for sinners to be justified from the curse of the law in the sight of God, than by the imputation of that righteousness long ago performed by, and still residing with, the Person of Jesus Christ." In describing the righteous work of Christ in the believer and to emphasise that any righteousness in the believer is still Christ's righteousness, Bunyan uses the example of parents and their children. The children are fed and clothed but though they eat the food and put on the garments, this is only possible because of their

---

[67] Ibid, p. 295.
[68] Ibid, p. 594 ff.
[69] Ibid, Vol. I, p. 300 ff.

parents' daily care and provisions. Thus the feeding and clothing is the parents' doing and not the children's, "so", says Bunyan, "the righteousness wherewith we stand just before God from the curse, still resides in Christ, not in us."[70] Bunyan rejects utterly the idea that justification is performed after faith and stresses time and time again the 'long ago' nature of the finality of imputed righteousness. Justification is before faith and not after faith but it is still justification by the means of faith because faith is the conveyor or instrument by which God makes the sinner aware of his justification in God's sight. Bunyan believes that if one does not stress the finished work of Christ in evangelism, then one cannot possibly tell sinners how they can be saved.

Robert Traill (1642-1716)

The time came when much Puritanism grew cold and took up a mid-way position between Arminianism and the Reformed faith and God called such as Robert Traill to lead the people back to a right understanding and experience of justification. Traill confessed that "all the great fundamentals of Christian truth, centre in this of justification", and saw the rapid growth of 'new divinity', the name he attached to the mixture of Calvinism and Arminianism which was coming into vogue in the 1690s, as being the natural results of abandoning his comprehensive, Reformed view of justification. Drop this, he said, then one soon drops the doctrine of atonement and when that is dropped, Christ's divinity will follow. The new divinity, Traill shows, leads to Arminianism and Arminianism leads to Socinianism. The doctrine of justification, Traill maintains, even for those who maintain a firm belief in Scripture as the only rule of the Christian's thought, "hath been, and will still be a stone of stumbling; as our Lord Jesus Himself was, and is, Romans 9:32, 33; 1 Peter 2:7, 8." He adds, "Law and gospel, faith and works, Christ's righteousness and our own, grace and debt, do equally divide all the matter. Crafty men may endeavour to blend and mix these things together in justification; but it is a vain attempt."[71]

---

[70] Ibid, p. 302. See John Armstrong's misapplied use of this quote in Part 1, Chapter 1.
[71] *The Doctrine of Justification Vindicated*, p. 334.

Justification

Obviously, the modern mixture of Reformed theology and Arminianism had not set in so much in Traill's day as it has nowadays. Traill can even testify that not one minister in the whole of London had left the path of a right understanding of justification such as he maintains in his book *The Doctrine of Justification Vindicated from the Charge of Antinomianism.* However, Traill bemoans the fact that the decay and degeneracy in the teaching on justification is becoming acute and the Puritanism of his day could no longer compare positively with that of the earliest Protestants and Puritans. He is obviously hurt by those who strive to mix Reformed teaching with Romanism and Arminianism and label those such as himself who stick to the old Protestant and Puritan paths as 'Antinomians'. Indeed, he quotes Christopher Fowler with sympathy who said "He that will not be Antichristian, must be called an Antinomian." Of the half-way men who accuse the Orthodox of being Antinomian, Traill quite turns the tables on them showing how they depart from a true understanding of the law and concluding, "And is it not somewhat strange, that men who have so much zeal against an Antinomian principle, have so much kindness for true Antinomianism in practice? He is dismayed to find that former Reformed men who seek a 'middle way' "have a greater kindness for that extreme they go half-way to, than for that which they go half-way from." He is particularly worried about those who claim that Christ's righteousness in us is a mere legal righteousness whereas we must develop an evangelical righteousness of our own to balance it off.[72] Of Christ's righteousness imputed to the justified-one, Traill says:

> 1. That Christ's righteousness is the only plea and answer of a sinner arraigned at God's bar for life and death.
> 2. This righteousness is imputed to no man but a believer.
> 3. When it is imputed by grace, and applied by faith, it immediately and eternally becomes the man's righteousness, before God, angels, men, and devils, Romans 8:33, 35, 38, 39. It is a righteousness that is

---

[72] Ibid, pp. 291, 292, 336, 337.

never lost, never taken away, never ineffectual; answereth all charges, and is attended with all grace.[73]

Nevertheless, Traill denies outright that the justified sinner is left alone after his legal justification to exercise faith, repentance and sincere obedience and thus, as it were, earn his justification backwards. Traill insists that:

We tell sinners, that Jesus Christ will surely welcome all that come to him; and as he will not cast them out for their sinfulness, in their nature and by, past life, so neither for their misery, in the want of such qualifications and graces that he only can give.

That we do hold forth the propitiation in Christ's blood, as the only thing to be in the eye of a man that would believe on Christ unto justification of life; and that by this faith alone a sinner is justified, and God is justified in doing so.

That God justifieth the ungodly, Romans 4:5 neither by making him godly before he justified him (*vide Andrew Fuller*), nor leaving him ungodly after he hath justified him (*vide our modern Neonomians*); but that the same grace that justifies him, doth immediately sanctify him (*vide those modern self-styled 'Moderate Calvinists' who teach otherwise*).

If for such doctrine we be called Antinomians, we are bold to say, that there is some ignorance of, or prejudice at the known Protestant doctrine, in the hearts of the reproachers."[74]

Considering the timing of justification, Traill again takes up the taunts of those who cry Antinomian for believing that "a sinner is actually justified before he be united to God by faith." Traill responds:

---

[73] Ibid, pp. 338, 339.
[74] Ibid, p. 320.

Justification

It is strange, that such as are charged with this, of all men do most press on sinners to believe on Jesus Christ, and urge the damnation threatened in the gospel upon all believers. That there is a decreed justification from eternity, particular and fixed as to all the elect, and a virtual perfect justification of all the redeemed, in and by the death and resurrection of Jesus Christ, Isaiah 53:11; Romans 4:25; Hebrews 9:26, 28 and 10:14, is not yet called in question by any amongst us; and more, is not craved, but that a sinner, for his actual justification, must lay hold on and plead this redemption in Christ's blood by faith.[75]

Summing up the faith of our Reformers concerning justification, we may conclude that for them justification is the classifying word in Scripture describing God's entire work of salvation in Christ for the elect. The scope of justification entails God's decreeing love for His people, predestination, union with Christ, atonement, reconciliation, forgiveness of sins, the reversal of condemnation guilt and punishment, faith, Christ's righteousness imputed, the New Birth, sanctification and glorification. This justification is not only before God but also before oneself, angels and men. In justification mercy and justice meet, pardon is given and guilt removed and the converted man of God is made meet to live a life of righteousness in Christ and in the Spirit. Nevertheless, as the eighteenth century opened, there was a marked departure amongst many Reformed Christians from the teaching of their fathers. Latitudinarianism, New Divinity, Wesleyanism, the General Baptists and mass evangelism of the Charles Finney kind coupled with various universal theories of the atonement became more and more common. This has resulted in the modern profane theory of justification which sees justification as a mere forensic declaration, leaving it to the sinner's agency to make it actual and complete. Part Three will deal with the Continental Reformers on justification.

---

[75] Ibid, p. 318.

Part Three
The Teaching of the Continental Reformers

Chapter 1

Wittenberg and Zurich

The Wittenberg Reformation

The fundamental question for Martin Luther (1483-1546) was, "How can a sinner be made righteous before God?" After years of wearing hair shirts, self-flagellation and creeping on all fours to the cross in true, Roman catholic piety, the words of Scripture "The just shall live by faith" transformed Luther's life. He was given to see this great truth written in sun-beams throughout the entire Bible. He discovered that God's justice is another way of saying God's grace, by means of which God makes the sinner just by imputing to him the justifying righteousness of Christ. Luther's book *The Seven Penitential Psalms*[76] has opened the eyes of many on justification who formerly considered the act merely as 'legal fiction'. Here Luther describes how David begged the Lord to deliver him from sin. David pleads with God to teach him and to quicken him in the ways of righteousness. He prays, "Father, I know it is not Thy way to consider an elect sinner merely theoretically just. Please make me really and truly just." Luther sums up the whole of Psalm 143 in the words, "Make me by thy grace truthful and righteous", explaining that David is not talking merely about the characteristics of God's grace which is according to truth

---

[76] *Die Sieben Bußpsalmen.*

Justification

and righteousness but he is speaking of, "The grace by which, for Christ's sake, He makes us truthful and righteous."

According to Luther, following the Scriptures, justification was far more than a mere legal pardon. The unjustified are dealt with by the law and condemned but the justified have the gospel to speak within them and guide them. Justification is thus removed from the legality of the law and placed in the liberty of grace. When commenting on Psalm 85:8 "I will hear what the Lord God will say unto me", Luther says, "In this phrase the difference between the Gospel and the Law is touched upon. The Law is the word of Moses to us, the Gospel on the other hand is the word of God in us. The former abides without; it speaks in figures and visible forecasts of things to happen. On the other hand, the latter comes to us within, and speaks of inward and spiritual things and of truth. This is because the Holy Spirit internally activates us to the truth of the gospel and enables us to live accordingly."

In *The Holy Spirit as the Bringer of True Righteousness*, Luther tells his congregation that when the papists hear of Christ in us, they become angry as they place Christ in Heaven and leave Him there and require the sinner to perform works of righteousness without Christ. The Holy Spirit's task, however, is to teach us that we are one body with Christ and are part of Christ's fullness and He becomes to us our all in all (Ephesians 1:22 ff.) and the Firstborn amongst many brethren. The pope will have Christ soaring above us, the Spirit will have Christ working within us. He reveals Christ and His righteousness as a reality to and for us,[77] showing us the way of true discipleship as God's justified children.[78]

When commenting on Galatians 5:5, 6 "For we through the Spirit wait for the hope of righteousness by faith", Luther argues that the truly justified man is not bound to any law in order to become or remain righteousness. The law and works of themselves make fleshly people but the Spirit and faith make spiritual people.[79] Whoever

---

[77] Ausgewählte Werke, Calvar Ausgabe, Band III, p. 187 ff.

[78] See *Der Heilige Geist als Geber echter Jüngerschaft; Der Heilige Geist als Wirker der Gottesgemeinschaft* (The Holy Spirit as Giver of Real Discipleship: The Holy Spirit as Motivater of Fellowship with God.)

[79] *Die Wahrheit der Glaubensgerechtichkeit* (The Truth of Justification by Faith), ibid, Galatians, Band VI, p. 333 ff.

tempts the Christian away from faith back to the law, receives God's judgment upon him. Our modern 'Reformed Neonomians' would call this 'Antinomian', but Luther is putting the law in its correct place where it drives sinners to Christ but does not take over Christ's work of creating righteous people. In Galatians 3:8 ff, Luther explains how Paul teaches that those who are justified by faith are the heirs of Abraham and not Moses and goes on to argue that when the Galatians were justified by faith, they ran well (Galatians 5:7) but those who sought righteousness via Moses and not Christ strove to hinder the work of Christ's righteousness in the Galatian believers. Such carnal persuasion, Paul tells us, "cometh not of him that calleth you." Luther is blunter. He calls those who wait until a person is converted by grace and then try to force him back to Sinai, 'godless botchers in righteousness' who give birth to 'theological freaks'.[80]

The Zurich Reformation

Ulrich Zwingli (1484-1531) began the Swiss Reformation and Henry Bullinger completed it. Zwingli was never truly Reformed on the doctrine of imputation and as he developed his doctrine of justification in his arguments against Purgatory, he is not easily understood by those unfamiliar with such debates. Furthermore, Zwingli's statesmanship and politics often marred his testimony. A Reformer who dies on the battlefield in a war he provoked can hardly be a model for finding peace with God. Nevertheless, Zwingli, within the historical and political limits of his age, has much sound teaching on justification which he sees not as a product of faith but as the contents of faith. He published little on the subject himself besides his *Zurich Disputation Vom Fegfür* (Article 57, On Purgatory) in which he argues that Purgatory was thought to make the sinner just enough for a resurrection in righteousness but Christ has already justified the sinner and Christ, the only righteous One, dwells within him and thus purgatory is superfluous. It neither helps the unjustified sinner as his doom is sealed, nor the justified elect whose salvation is already assured. After Zwingli's death, Bullinger published Zwingli's *Erklärung des Christlichen Glaubens* (Exposition of the Faith) in 1536. A similar version in French was soon published by Calvin, the

---

[80] Commentary on Galatians 5:2.

Justification

first edition of his ever expanding major compilation of theology called *The Institutes*. In his brief systematic theology, Zwingli argues that justifying faith and good works are the natural consequence of election. Therefore though Christian works are not meritorious, they are the natural work of God in the believer who walks by faith believing Christ's promise in John 14:12 "Verily, verily I say unto you, he that believeth on me, the works that I shall do shall he do also, and greater works than these shall he do." Another text Zwingli gives is Matthew 7:20, "If ye have faith as a grain of mustard seed, ye shall say unto this mountain, Remove hence to yonder place; and it shall remove and nothing shall be impossible unto you."[81]

Henry Bullinger (1504-1575) perhaps the most able early teacher on justification, taught that an understanding of both the imputation of Adam's sin to all mankind and the imputation of Christ's righteousness to all the elect was fundamental to a correct, Biblical view of justification. Bullinger explains in his *Second Helvetic Confession* that:

> To justify, in the apostle's disputation touching justification, does signify to remit sins, to absolve from the fault and the punishment thereof, to receive into favour, to pronounce a man just.

This comprehensive view of justification was faithfully presented as the only Reformed view of justification possible until recent years. Today Philipp Melanchthon's view of a purely legal 'as if' teaching on justification has rid this basic Reformation doctrine of all its gospel spirituality. Bullinger goes on to explain that because of the justifying results of Christ's work "He imputes the justice of Christ unto us for our own; so that we are not only cleansed from sin, and purged and holy, but also endued with the righteousness of Christ; yea, and acquitted from sin, death, and condemnation." This faith, Bullinger argues, is not:

---

[81] Zwingli's *Works*, Vol. 11, p. 343. See Bromiley's English SCM translation, p. 272.

a feigned, vain or dead faith, but of a lively and quickening faith; which, for Christ (who is life, and gives life), whom it apprehends, both is indeed, and is so called, a lively faith, and does prove itself to be lively by lively works. And, therefore, James does speak nothing contrary to this doctrine; for he speaks of a vain and dead faith, which certain bragged of, but had not Christ living within them by faith. And also James says that works do justify (chapter 2:14, 26), yet he is not contrary to Paul (for then he were to be rejected); but he shows that Abraham did declare his lively and justifying faith by works. And so do all the godly, who yet do trust in Christ alone, not to their own works. For the apostle said again, "Nevertheless I live; yet not I but Christ liveth in me: and the life which I now live in the flesh, I live by the faith of the Son of God who loved me, and gave himself for me. I do not frustrate the grace of God; for if righteousness come by the law, then Christ is dead in vain (Galatians 2:20, 21).

True, Reformed justification is no longer preached in most so-called Reformed pulpits and the Church of the Lord Jesus Christ needs a new Luther and a new Bullinger to bring back our lost Reformation. Bullinger's *Decades* once compulsory reading for Anglican theological students, are full of teaching on justification. For Bullinger, justification per definition means "to quit from judgment and from the denounced and uttered sentence of condemnation. It signifieth to remit offences, to cleanse, to sanctify, and to give inheritance of life everlasting." Further, he says that justification stands for "the absolution and remission of sins, for sanctification, and adoption into the number of the sons of God." It is a work done by God as a free gift which was not possible to be attained through the law of Moses (Acts 13:38, 39). Bullinger sees justification as synonymous with forgiveness of sins, sanctification and adoption, all ordained in the electing courts of God and wrought out for us through the Saviour. His doctrine is thus justification according to "the eternal

Justification

and unchangeable will of God", described in Ephesians 2:8-10 as "By grace are ye saved through faith, and that is not of yourselves; it is the gift of God: not of works, lest any man should boast himself. For we are the workmanship of God, created in Christ Jesus into good works, which God hath before ordained that we should walk in them." Justification, Bullinger teaches, is not the work of a second when the believer comes to Christ but it is another term for everlasting life and the inseparable corollary of bringing forth righteous fruits, i.e. sanctification and holiness, which are part and parcel of justification and not separate gifts or merits. It is only when these truths are preached and followed, says Bullinger, that we serve God as we ought.[82]

---

[82] *Decades*, Vol. 1, pp. 104, 121

Chapter 2

Strasburg and Geneva

Fathering 'Calvinism'

Martin Bucer (1491-1553) and John Calvin (1509-1564) must be considered together in accessing what has come to be called 'Calvinism' amongst Reformed people. Many Reformed scholars claim that Calvin's doctrines are unique, his writings are the nearest to Scripture and Geneva cradled the Reformation. This picture fails to give due credit to the Strasburg and Zurich sources from which Calvin gained his doctrines and church order.

Our churches appear unaware of the enormous part Bucer and Strasburg played in the Genevan Reformation. M. van Campen thus rightly calls Bucer 'the forgotten Reformer'.[83] Pick up Calvin's *Institutes* where you will and Bucer's thoughts are revealed almost verbatim, including at times sections and subsections. Whenever we speak of the Reformed faith in terms of election, predestination, the Holy Spirit, the Church, church-state relationships, church discipline, church offices, liturgies, ordinances, marriage or even mundane aspects of life such as banking and commerce, we are speaking of doctrines and disciplines which Calvin gained from Bucer previous to and during his 1538-43 exile in the city. Indeed, two major editions of *The Institutes* and Calvin's first major commentaries were published in Strasburg. Bucer introduced Calvin to the art of diplomacy and church administration and took him to the great church conferences at

---

[83] *Martin Bucer: een vergeten reformator*, 's-Gravenhage, 1991.

Justification

Worms and Regensburg to learn the art of debating. Even in family matters, Calvin was strongly influenced by Bucer who told the Frenchman that he needed a wife and introduced him to Idelette de Bure whom Calvin quickly married. Indeed, Calvin seems to have had no thought of returning to Geneva and took out Strasburg citizenship in 1540. All this leads Gustav Anrich to claim that Calvin merely stood on Bucer's shoulders and that Bucer was the true 'father of Calvinism'.[84]

Revived interest in Bucer

Happily Bucer is being rediscovered. Reformed seminaries have been founded at Bonn and Hamburg to promote the great reforming doctrines of this pastor-scholar, and an institute for Bucer Studies has been established at Heidelberg where the Reformer's works are being translated and published by an international team of experts. The year 2001 was the 450th anniversary of Bucer's death and Bonn's Martin Bucer Seminary publish a memorial year-book entitled *Anwalt der Liebe: Martin Bucer als Theologe and Seelsorger*[85] in which Prof. Thomas Schirrmacher demonstrates that Calvin became a Calvinist through Bucer.[86] Christian magazines such as *New Focus* and the *Banner of Truth* have recently issued articles on Bucer's pioneering work.[87]

The relationship between Bucer and Calvin was similar to that of Luther and Melanchthon. Luther was the greater evangelist and the better theologian but Melanchthon had a greater talent for consolidating and organizing the work. Calvin, as Bucer's Melanchthon, took Bucer's evangelical doctrines to what he thought was their logical conclusion. He made them, according to Anrich, 'härter und schroffer' (harsher and blunter); more suitable for the lawyer and the lecture hall rather than the caring pastor or the seeking sinner. Bucer and his French-speaking colleague Valerand Poullain maintained that church order and discipline were utility measures prescribed by the apostles and did not tie a church down to a fixed

---

[84] *Martin Bucer*, Strasburg, 1914, p. 143, 144.

[85] *Advocate of Love: Martin Bucer as Theologian and Carer of Souls.*

[86] *Anwalt der Liebe*, p. 51, Bonn, 2001.

[87] *New Focus*, 'Martin Bucer: Moderator of the Reformation', December/January 2002; *Banner of Truth*, Martin Bucer (1491-1551), Parts I and II, October and November 2001.

go *Topical*

hierarchy if local conditions hindered this. They thus gave great latitude to alternative forms. When Calvin was ejected from Geneva, and found asylum in Bucer's Strasburg, he adopted the Strasburg Order and introduced it to his flock on returning to Geneva in 1543. The resulting Genevan Order was a sharpening, regulating, and formalising of the original.

Tolerant Bucer worshipped side by side with Lutheran, Presbyterian, Episcopalian and a number of Separatist churches whereas Calvin felt uncomfortable outside the four walls of Geneva and took little part in discussions with Nonconformists. Nor did Calvin share Bucer's vision for world-wide evangelism and missions. Bucer supported Cranmer, Alasco and other great Reformers in campaigning for an international Reformed Church, incorporating European-wide Reformed theology, whereas Calvin and Beza viewed their local Genevan church, with all its shortcomings as a fitting model for all to join.

Bucer presents justification as an integral unity but Calvin, who otherwise follows him closely, sees justification as a paradox. This has caused both those who claim that justification is merely forensic and, paradoxically, those who believe justification actively changes the inner being to quote Calvin as their authority. This writer believes that Calvin is very close to Bucer but Bucer expresses his doctrine of justification in the general comprehensive, pastoral phraseology of the earlier Reformation, whereas, Calvin in consolidating and systematising justification majored more on its passive rather than its active or rather activating side.[88] Calvinists who believe that Calvin did not link justification with predestination and viewed the doctrine of justification as a legal freedom from condemnation only, tend to stress the human, active side of justification in an Amyraldian and Neonomian way.

Calvin's teaching on justification developed through strife
Calvin sets his teaching on justification in the *Institutes* against the background of his highly polemic debates with Andreas Osiander (1498-1565) who believed that an 'essential righteousness' preceded justification. Osiander, pioneer of the Nürnberg Reformation, opposed

---

[88] See Berkhof's *Systematic Theology*, p. 514 ff..

Justification

the Genevan school with great heat. Calvin replied with the same vigour, abandoning much of what he had in common with Osiander in his attack. Osiander appears quite orthodox on justification until we examine him on its forensic nature, the imputed righteousness of Christ and the work of Christ in the believer. He dismissed the idea that justification was a mere annulling of past sins; a mere declaration of justification without any changing, active influence on the justified one and argued that a justification without fruit in the life of the believer was unthinkable. This correct analysis led him strangely to a wrong conclusion. He argued that we are not really justified as ungodly but that Christ indwells us first, then infuses His righteousness in us to make us essentially righteous and ripe for God's pronouncement of justification. Osiander viewed the indwelling Christ as the infusion of Christ's righteousness in the believer making him a mystical participator in the divine nature. Thus, when God justifies, He does so on the grounds that the sinner has already been given an essentially just nature. Osiander thus believed in two kinds of righteousness: the righteousness imputed by Christ which was Christ's everlasting righteousness as God, and the righteousness which Christ wrought out in obeying the law as a Man among men. Calvin saw rightly that this did away with the need for Christ's incarnation, vicarious death and resurrection. The Scriptures do testify to our being partakers of Christ and His holiness, as also partakers of the Holy Spirit and even partakers of the divine nature, but this is only because we have been given "all things that pertain unto life and godliness, through the knowledge of him that hath called us to glory and virtue."[89] These gifts were given to the elect sinner according to Scripture whilst he was yet ungodly and by virtue of Christ's sacrificial and vicarious death.[90]

Calvin, however, is nearer Osiander than Bucer, Bullinger and the English Reformers in his order of justification. He places regeneration chronologically before justification,[91] interpreting justification by faith as a justification which ensues because of faith given. Regeneration

---

[89] Hebrews 2:14; Hebrews 12:10; Hebrews 6:4; 2 Peter 1:4.
[90] Romans 4:5; 5:6.
[91] *Institutes*, Vol. 1, Book III, Chapter III, p. 508 ff.. See especially Vol. 2, Book III, Chapter XI, p. 37.

brings the life of believers into concord and harmony with the righteousness of God.[92] Justification is the confirmation of this righteous faith given to the elect.[93] Calvin's order is therefore, regeneration, faith, repentance, justification. Calvin adopted this view to ensure that justification was seen as coming via faith, but it jeopardises the Biblical doctrine that God justifies the sinner whilst he is at enmity with God (Romans 4:5; 5:9, 10).

Neither Bucer nor Calvin separated sanctification and holiness from justification, denying that God's justification was an act without consequences in the believer. They emphasised Romans 6:18, "Being thus made free from sin, ye became the servants of righteousness", stressing that both aspects belong to the one justification.

Views concerning a double justification

Calvin adopted Bucer's belief in a double predestination but Bucer believed also in what is faultily called a double justification. He taught firstly that justification for the elect is solely through God's predestinating grace. One cannot therefore think in terms of a justification separated from electing mercies. Secondly, Bucer maintained that though justification was imputed passively to the yet ungodly elect in the Pauline sense, that same justification produced an active outworking in the life of the justified, one in the sense of James' teaching in his epistle. With the accounting of a person as righteous comes also the announcement to that person's consciousness that he is justified. This justification, however, is not only a declaration but a transformation. It changes man, turns him about and sets him upon the path of the just. An alleged just man who cannot bring forth fruits of justification is not a justified man. This was the same doctrine that England's early Reformers Robert Barnes and Miles Coverdale taught, arguing that if an Antinomian claims that he need do no good works because he is justified by faith, such a man has neither faith nor is justified.[94] Such fruits, however, are not the works of natural man but stem from the justifying mercies of God in Christ who now indwells man and guides him by His Spirit. Thus forensic

---

[92] Vol. 2, Book III, Chapter VI, 1, p. 2.
[93] Vol. 2, Book III, Chapter XI, p. 36.
[94] Parker Society, *2 Coverdale*, p. 341 and Index pp. 451, 452.

Justification

justification is inseparable from effective justification which is not a condition for being justified or a second justification, but the result of being justified. It is thus incorrect to speak of a double justification in Bucer's theology as the two aspects of justification go hand in hand and complement each other. Those who separate sanctification and holiness from justification are certainly in danger of regarding justification as being in two stages. One from God's side and one from man's.

Wilhelm Niesel in his thought-provoking book *The Theology of Calvin*, suggests, leaning on *Institutes*, Book III, Chapter XVII, 4, 5, that Calvin held to a dual form of justification in order to harmonise divergent Scripture texts. He argues that Calvin thus distinguished between "justification granted to man in his estrangement from God and the justification which the believer needs during his lifetime. Hence there is a justification which pays no regard to the works of man and a justification in regard to which works are considered as the fruits of faith."[95] However, a careful study of these passages clearly shows that Niesel has confused Calvin's own view with the one he is refuting at the time. Holiness, for Calvin, is not a second works-orientated justification but it is grounded in the one justification by grace and is manifested in its works.

Calvin teaches that the holiness which is the believer's after justification cannot be separated from the imputed righteousness of Christ which is given him[96] and that this justification is not merely passive but actually operative,[97] thus practical holiness and sanctification are inseparable from justification. When God sanctifies us in Christ, He justifies us. There is no justification without sanctification.[98] He also clearly links predestination, adoption and being accepted in the Beloved.[99] In keeping with the bulk of the Reformers, Calvin also stresses that not only is the righteousness of Christ imputed to the elect sinner, but also justification brings with it, indeed, consists in, the forgiveness of sins.[100] This is why Calvin can

---

[95] Chapter Nine, The Grace of God Within Us, p. 135.
[96] Vol. 1, Book III, Chapter III, 1, p. 509.
[97] Vol. 2, Book III, Chapter XVII, 12, p. 115.
[98] Vol. 2, Book III, Chapter XVI, 1, pp. 98, 99.
[99] Vol. 2, Book III, Chapter XI, 4, pp. 39, 40.
[100] Vol. 2, Book III, Chapter XI, 2, p. 38.

say in Book III, Chapter XI, 1, that the doctrine of justification is "the principle ground on which religion must be supported." Sadly, such a comprehensive grasp of Biblical justification is quite absent from the bulk of modern Reformed evangelism, preaching and teaching.

Justification

Chapter 3

The Dutch Nadere Reformatie (Continuing Reformation)

The English and German speaking churches are now re-discovering the Dutch Puritans with whom they worked so closely in the 17th and 18th Centuries but from whom they have departed during the last two centuries. The Puritan movement in the Netherlands was called the Nadere Reformatie which was unhappily translated into The Second Reformation by English and American writers. This is a total misnomer which suggests that the Nadere Reformatie cannot be identified with the 16th Century Reformation and, indeed, went a totally different way. The word 'nadere', however, means 'at hand' or 'near' and would be better translated with 'Reformation at Hand' or 'Reformation Now'. Actually, the men of this Dutch movement which included Britain's ex-patriots William Ames (1576-1633) and Alexander Comrie (1708-1774), looked upon the Nadere Reformatie as a Continuous Reformation and this term describes the aims of the movement far better than the misleading 'Second Reformation'. The best known representative of the Nadere Reformatie amongst English-speaking readers is undoubtedly Herman Witsius (1636-1708). The Reformed movement started off with a concentrated focus on Christian doctrine and experience but gradually became broader in its views absorbing both Lutheran pietism (as opposed to the Reformed Pietism of the Untereyck school) and a formal philosophical legalism. The latter development was due to what Joel Beeke has defined as 'meticulous doctrinal analysis'[101] and the practice of viewing faith, holiness and sanctification by means of syllogisms based on one's individual experience as a means of testing how one is growing in

---

[101] *The Christian's Reasonable Service*, Wilhelmus à Brakel, The Essence of the Dutch Second Reformation, p. lxxxviii.

grace. In other words, the Dutch development directly paralleled that in the English-speaking countries at the time. The movement away from a spontaneous and comprehensive experience of Christian doctrine towards an analytical separating of doctrines from their attributes and fruits can be seen when comparing the two Nadere Reformatie stalwarts mentioned below.[102]

Herman Faukel the Dutch Catechist (1560-1625)

The work of this Dutch divine was centred in Reformed orthodoxy and similar to that of his English predecessor Alexander Nowell. Faukel presented to his church a catechism which was fully didactic and Scriptural, suitable for young communicants and trainee clergy alike. Unlike Nowell who worked mostly from his own earlier concepts, Faukel based his work on the Heidelberg Catechism. Not only is this catechism still widely used in Continental Europe and regularly reprinted, the Dutch version, and other catechisms based on it, is still published with Faukel's *Brief Sketch of the Christian Religion.*[103]

The *Brief Sketch* is a summary of the Heidelberg Catechism in the usual question and answer style. It came into being in 1611, the year of the English King James' Version of the Scriptures, when the Synod of Veere decided to issue a new edition of the Heidelberg Catechism, the Dutch Confession of Faith and the Dutch Reformed Liturgy. Since then, Faukel's work has its permanent place in the confessions of the Dutch Reformed churches.

The work starts with three questions addressed to the young convert or communicant, namely, how great is our sin and spiritual poverty; how can we be freed from our sins and how can we thank God for our salvation. These questions, divided into numerous subquestions and answers are all exemplified by copious Bible texts.

---

[102] I am greatly indebted to Volker Jordan of the Friends of the Heidelberg Catechism and Dort for introducing me to Faulkel and Hellenbroek. Jordan has recently translated their catechetical and dogmatic works into German. It is worthwhile, however, learning Dutch at least passively as there is a great fullness of sound Christian literature in that language which rivals the best of the English-speaking world. There have been correspondingly great works in German but lack of interest has caused many of them to have faded out of existence. It appears to be impossible to find German publishers interested in finding and reprinting old spiritual treasures.

[103] *Kort Begrip der Christelijke Religie met Uitgeschreven Bewijsteksten,* Gereformeerde Bijbelsstichting, 2001.

Faukel develops his doctrine of justification against the background of Christ's mediatory role on behalf of His elect. This role he sees as starting in the eternal covenant of the Father with the Son and Holy Spirit regarding the salvation of His people. It is thus to be expected that Faukel makes much of Romans 8:30, "Whom he did predestinate, them he also called: and whom he called, them he also justified: and whom he justified, them he also glorified." Here the Dutch Bible uses the present perfect tense which both emphasises the finished aspect of such work with its continuing, indeed, eternal consequences and the economy of the blessings irrespective of time sequence. Needless to say, Faukel links Romans 8:30 with Ephesians 1:4, "According as he hath chosen us in him before the foundation of the world, that we should be holy and without blame before him in love." These truths cause Faukel to affirm that justification entails not only being adjudged free from condemnation and guilt but also receiving a new life of sanctification from God with the promise that the believer will be kept in the faith which has been given to him. Thus the decree of justification includes not only the declarative but also the transformative mercies of God.

When discussing the purpose of Christ's death and resurrection, Faukel stresses, quoting Romans 4:25, this was so that Christ's Bride might be justified. He saw this justification as being by faith but not a faith produced by the sinner because this is beyond fallen man's ability. The faith which Christ requires is not faith which comes by the law as a work of man but faith which comes by grace which is Christ's work. To illustrate this point, Faukel quotes Galatians 2:16, "Knowing that a man is not justified by the works of the law, but by the faith of Jesus Christ, that we might be justified by the faith of Christ, and not by the works of the law: for by the works of the law shall no flesh be justified." He forces this home by quoting, amongst other texts, Ephesians 2:8, "For by grace we are saved, through faith; and that not of ourselves: it is the gift of God."

Abraham Hellenbroek (1658-1731): Making Voetius and Cocceius meet

Hellenbroek studied at Leiden before becoming a minister of the gospel at Zwammerdam in 1683, followed by pastorates at

Justification

Zwijndrecht (1691), Zaltbommel (1694) and Rotterdam (1695). He was strongly influenced by Gysbertus Voetius (1588-1676) the famous Utrecht professor and High Calvinist who fought bitterly against the greater tolerance of Johannes Koch (Cocceius) of Bremen (1603-1669) though Koch also influenced the Nadere Reformatie greatly. Koch criticised the scholastic orthodoxy of the Gomarus-Voetius school, claiming that it was orthodox by name but worldly by nature. Doctrine, he argued, was useless unless accompanied by personal piety and love and tolerance for others. Though he emphasised that God was the Giver and man the receiver in matters of grace, he emphasised more the responsibility of the believer to 'work out his own salvation', knowing that he was in the will of God. Hellenbroek has the same predestinarian teaching of Voetius but, like the greater Witsius, took his covenant teaching and personal piety from Koch. Hellenbroek's failing, if he had any failings at all, was to place Cocceian piety under the analytical formalism of Voetius, thus ridding theology of some of the freshness and spontaneity advocated by Koch.

Hellenbroek's teaching on justification is found in his *Voorbeeld der Goddelijke Waarheden Voor Eenvoudigen.*[104] This typically pietistic title might be translated as *Examples of Godly Truths for the Simple-Hearted.* The book is intended for newcomers to the faith and takes them through the major doctrines of the Bible. The language is clear and simple, yet it carries such profound thoughts that it is still widely used in Holland for catechizing their youth.

Chapter XV of *Examples of Godly Truths* is entitled On Justification and opens with the question whether or not all those who receive an inner call from God are justified. His answer is taken from Romans 8:30 explaining that those who God predestinates to salvation are called, justified and glorified. His definition of justification is based on Romans 4:7 and 5:19. Justification entails the annulment of guilt and punishment and forgiveness of sins through the vicarious obedience of Christ. Unlike many of his Reformed predecessors, Hellenbroek insists that there are three reasons for distinguishing sharply between justification and sanctification. 1. Justification is

---

[104] *Voorbeeld der Goddelijke Waarheden Voor Eenvoudigen, die Zich Bereiden tot Belijdenis des Geloofs. Uitgebreid met Volledige Bijbelteksten,* Uitgeverij de Banier, 2001.

external to man whereas sanctification is internal. 2. Justification removes guilt but sanctification the stains of sin. 3. Justification is once and for all time but sanctification is progressive. This leaves Hellenbroek to conclude that there is no internal change in the sinner on being pronounced justified but this is wrought out after the event by sanctification. Thus, for Hellenbroek, justification is merely declarative and not transformative. This view is open to criticism. 1. Hellenbroek's teaching that sanctification takes away the stain of sin stands in sharp contrast to his belief that justification removes guilt and brings with it the forgiveness of sins. 2. Hellenbroek provides rich testimony from the Scriptures of evidence of what he calls 'external justification' but his definitions of internal sanctification are merely stated as opinions without Scriptural backing. 3. The fact that sanctification is progressive does not rule out the fact that Christ's justifying work in the sinner makes him a new creature, fitted out for good works. Nevertheless, Hellenbroek remains convinced that justification "is only a sentence or acquittal pronounced as a judge in court". However, Hellenbroek immediately modifies what he has so dogmatically said by claiming that in the process of justification, the Father as judge pronounces the sinner free of guilt, the Son takes on the office of Mediator and Defender and the Holy Spirit seals our justification, gives us both knowledge of it and assurance that it is ours. Here we see the folly of viewing justification formally and externally as one thing and its fruits formally and internally as another. When one comes to the practical application of justification, it is immediately obvious that justification and sanctification cannot be separated. There is no justification without sanctification and no sanctification without justification. Actually, if Hellenbroek had followed Koch a little more, he would have seen that justification belongs to God's post legal economy of the covenant which is the government of grace and not law.[105]

Concerning the origins of faith in the justified, Hellenbroek returns to good Biblical data. On asking the question how are the blessings of justification reckoned to us, quoting Romans 3:24, he answers that this accounting righteous is a free gift in accordance with grace through

---

[105] Koch distinguished between the ant- legal, the legal and the post-legal aspects of the divine economy of grace.

Justification

the atoning work of Christ. Then comes the question, how can this grace be received? The answer is 'by faith' but this faith, Hellenbroek explains, is found outlined in Philippians 3:9, "not having mine own righteousness, which is of the law, but that which is through the faith of Christ, the righteousness which is of God by faith." Thus justifying faith is not the faith of the believer worked out by law righteousness but the faith of Christ imputed to us by grace. Hellenbroek then asks if we are justified because of our faith. His answer is in the negative. He affirms that the Scriptures speak only of 'from faith' or 'through faith' but not 'because of faith'. Hellenbroek answers the question, "Cannot we believe of ourselves?" with a firm "No", quoting Ephesians 2:8, "For by grace are ye saved through faith; and that not of yourselves: it is the gift of God." Hellenbroek's last question in this section is "What function has faith in this connection?" He replies, "It serves as a hand or instrument by which we receive the merits of Christ." This truth is worked out in detail in Hellenbroek's following chapter *On Faith* in which he asks who works this faith in us. He takes his answer from 1 Corinthians 12:3; Philippians 1:19 and Galatians 5:22 which refer to the work of the Holy Spirit in the justified one.

Herman Witsius (1636-1708): Man of the Covenant
Witsius taught that God who never changes has covenanted with His Son in eternity to seek out a people for Himself to make them partakers of His divine, perfect, unalterable and eternal nature. For him, the doctrine of justification was the key to this covenant as far as it concerns the people of God's choice.

Witsius was born of believing parents who, like Hannah and Elkanah committed their son to God before his birth. He learnt to know and commune with the Lord from an early age and received the best education possible at the time from his learned uncle, Peter Gerhard. At the age of fourteen, after being trained in History, Dutch, French, Latin, Greek, Hebrew and Science by Gerhard but also in the ways of the Lord, Herman entered Utrecht University. Whilst studying under Hoornbek, Voetius and Bogaerdtius Herman came to a saving knowledge of Christ.

At the age of nineteen, Witsius was called to pastor a French-speaking church and soon after, at West Wouden, he wrote a treatise on the Trinity which found international acclamation. He then engaged on an itinerant ministry through which many people, especially amongst the youth, came to faith in Christ.

After 1660 Witsius, now married, was invited to church after church which was going through internal troubles and he always brought peace and unity to them. When the War of Independence broke out in 1672, Witsius was amazed to find that England, the land of the Puritans, had turned tail and, under Charles II, was supporting Louis XIV of France against the United Provinces. Just as the Netherlands were about to be trodden underfoot, William of Orange was raised up to save the Dutch from disaster and the English from shame and both Holland and England from a Papal take-over.

Gaining his doctor's degree in 1675, Witsius was called to the Chair of Theology at Franeker University where he taught the truths of Scripture against Rome and Dutch Protestants such as Grotius who had rejected a sola scriptura theology in exchange for an institutionalised, sacramental view of the church based on tradition which they called the *pia antiquitas* and which paved the way back to Rome. Grotius, whose teaching is known to the English-speaking world through American New Divinity and English Fullerism, spoke of a 'law' which was not the Law of Moses and a 'satisfaction' which was not through punishment and a 'substitution' which was not of necessity and not vicarious.[106] His work against Rome, Socinianism, Grotianism and Arminianism gave rise to Witsius' *Economy of the Covenants*. Witsius' work was re-issued in England in the following century by John Gill which is the edition currently available through the den Dulk Christian Foundation with an Introduction by J. I. Packer. When James Hervey was sent the Gill edition by John Ryland Sen. in February, 1753, he wrote to a friend, saying "I wish, for my own sake, that you was somewhat acquainted with the author, because, if you should be inclined to know the reason and foundation of my sentiments on any particular point, Witsius might be my spokesman; he would declare my mind better than I could do myself." In his famous work *Theron and Aspasio*, Hervey calls Witsius' work "the golden pot which had manna; and was outwardly bright with burnished gold; inwardly rich with heavenly food."

---

[106] One can draw close parallels with Andrew Fuller and Hugo Grotius here.

Justification

Witsius' energies were enormous. He seemed to work day and night, preaching, writing and teaching so that his friends affirmed that he never slept. Indeed, Witsius is known to have often worked through several days and nights without a wink of sleep even when middle aged. His fame led to his being sent as a leading member of a Dutch delegation to the court of James II of England in 1685 in an effort to turn the King from Rome to the Reformed faith. During the months Witsius spent in England he pleased all denominations by treating both Anglicans and Dissenters on equal terms and had sweet fellowship with evangelicals of both parties. He was made Chancellor of Utrecht University in 1686.

When the great Antinomian-Neonomian Controversy spread through Britain, destroying the churches, Witsius was invited to take on the role of Moderator by all sides. This gave rise to Witsius' work *Conciliatory Animadversions on the Controversies agitated in Britain under the Names of Antinomians and Neonomians.*[107] Witsius was surprised by the lack of Biblical understanding shown both by the alleged Antinomians and their alleged Neonomian brethren, particularly regarding election and justification. Both sides had seemingly no Biblical idea of eternity and had looked upon eternal election as God's will declared in an age before our age or in some other form of past time. They could not conceive as Witsius and Scripture that God is working His purpose out from eternity and this purpose is manifested in God's all-presence in time.

Witsius gained a personal friend in William of Orange and was able to influence him strongly in gospel matters. In 1698 William asked Witsius as a personal favour to take over the Chair of Divinity at Leyden. Old age was now rapidly taking its toll of Witsius' health as he had never spared himself and he felt he should obey the call and now concentrate on preparing men for the ministry, giving up pastoral work. A year later, Witsius was elected Regent of a theological college set up by the Dutch States and West Friesland, and again Witsius found himself with a dual burden as Leyden begged him to stay. Though Witsius was rapidly fading from this world, his fame was still growing and seekers after righteousness and true learning

---

[107] I have not been able to date this moderating work exactly but it probably occurred in 1685 when Witsius was for a short time chaplain to the embassy of the Dutch Provinces in London.

flocked to him from all the Dutch States, France, Germany, England, Poland, Switzerland and Eastern Europe. Even American Indians, converted through the work of John Eliot (1604-90) and those who followed him, found their way to Leyden to be trained for the ministry.

Witsius' last six years were spent in acute pain and dizziness. He suffered from severe memory lapses and at times he quite lost his powers of thought. After a serious attack in October, 1708, Witsius told those at his side that his home-call had come. He spent the last hour of his life speaking of his blessed hope and heavenly joys before peacefully closing his eyes to be awakened in Glory.

Witsius outlined his doctrine of justification in his *Economy of the Covenants*. His teaching is perhaps the most complicated system of justification of all Reformed writers. He is often guilty of over-meticulous doctrinal analysis. His basic stand is that justification is an essential part of the covenant of grace which is secured in Christ outside of time, that is, in eternity. This eternal decree is operated in time from eternity in various 'articles'[108] or periods in the history of salvation. He speaks of a general justification of the elect but also of their particular justification depending on whether or not he is looking from the point of view of eternity or time.

The first period refers to justification through the "suretyship of Christ, whereby he took upon himself all the sins of the elect, and on account of which God declared, he never intended to exact them from any of his chosen; because, on admitting a Surety, the principle debtor is freed from all obligation to make satisfaction. And this is the first effect of Christ's suretyship, the declaration of that counsel of God, by which he had purposed to justify the ungodly; and not impute sin to those who are inserted as heirs in the testament." Witsius argues that this part of the divine plan of justification was effected when it was needed, i.e. after the fall. It was an infralapsarian plan which was effected as soon as man sinned. Witsius argues in this way as there was no need for justification to absolve man until man sinned in Adam his federal head.

Witsius' second period of general justification was when "God was in Christ, reconciling the world unto himself, not imputing their

---

[108] Witsius' own term.

Justification

trespasses unto them" (2 Corinthians 5:19). Witsius takes 'the world' here to be the world of the elect, and non-imputation is, for him, justification. He thus sees justification as akin to the forgiveness of sin and reconciliation with God through union with Christ.

The third period for Witsius is at conversion when the elect person receives a living faith and the application of justification hitherto reserved for him in Christ. He is now declared pardoned in the court of heaven and free from God's wrath and placed in God's special favour.

The fourth stage is the outworking of the gift of faith on the conscience of the pardoned one so that the believer knows, feels and experiences that he is justified. The believer is thus actively justified when he was yet ungodly and passively justified when faith was given him. This is an important factor to note as modern Hyper-Calvinist hunters look upon the doctrine of passive and active justification as a symbol of supralapsarianism and thus Hyper-Calvinism. Both Witsius and Gill, however were sub or infralapsarians, yet they held to an active and passive doctrine of justification.

The fifth stage for Witsius comes when the believer is admitted to a 'familiar converse with God' and real joy in believing ensues.

The sixth stage arrives when at death, the elect are received by God and the seventh follows at the day of judgment when the elect will be publicly justified and declared heirs of eternal life.

One could sum up Witsius' view of justification in the words, "God is always declaring his elect to be just and is thus always making His elect just, blending legal fulfilment in union with Christ with the righteousness of grace." Witsius' remarks are thus not to be understood merely chronologically but as the outworkings of God's covenant economy for His people throughout eternity, hence the title of his book. Thus the foundation of justification is eternity, embracing "the righteousness of Christ the Lord, communicated to them (the elect) according to the free decrees of election, which is succeeded by adoption, which gives them a right to take possession of the inheritance."

Here, Witsius, distinguishes between the bare declaration of justification and the making of the justified true to their justified state. Indeed, Witsius argues from the Greek and Hebrew that the Biblical terms mean 'to make true', in other words, to be conformed to the true image of God by the grace of the Spirit and the indwelling Lord. He can thus speak of the grounds of God's accepting the elect as 'true' (i.e. righteous) as the effects of divine grace in their lives, proved by faith and good works. Indeed, Witsius does not hesitate to use the term 'inherent righteousness' here, i.e. a righteousness communicated by the Spirit of sanctification, arguing that one cannot separate the declaration of justification in the process of justification from its effects. [109]

Gill, who popularized Witsius amongst the English-speaking churches, obviously leaned heavily on his mentor in his treatment of justification but strove to simplify him on the tripartite lines of traditional British Reformed thinking.

Part Four will sum up the previous parts in the light of Scripture.

---

[109] See *Economy of the Covenants*, Vol. I, Book III, Chapter VIII, Of Justification, pp. 391, 428.

Justification

Part Four
Unrighteousness Made Righteous

Chapter 1

What Saith the Scripture?

Justification from all claims of the law

A widespread modern evangelical view regarding justification is that it is merely a legal term signifying a forensic act with no causative or generative properties on behalf of the person justified. The sinner is merely declared to be just but left as he is. The term 'justification' is thus used as the opposite of the term 'condemnation'. Just as the sinner is legally condemned, it is argued, so the believer is legally justified in that the charges against him are dropped. This purely judicial understanding of justification was adopted and developed by Melanchthon whilst systematizing, contracting and classifying Luther's far more dynamic and comprehensive doctrine. The grave theological and judicial weaknesses in this theory are immediately apparent.

The Mosaic law is the only law which the sinner must face for his condemnation but he must look elsewhere for his justification. It is true that the Mosaic law condemns us but it is not true that the Mosaic law justifies us. Sinners deserve to be condemned but they do not deserve to be justified. Christ's justification is different from Moses' condemnation. Paul indeed says in Galatians 2:21, "If righteousness come by the law, then Christ is dead in vain." There is no justification by law for sinful man but a justifying deliverance from the condemnation of the law wrought by grace. The justification of a

Justification

believer, the Bible tell us, is a justification "from all things, from which ye could not be justified by the law of Moses" (Acts 13:39). Indeed, the Scriptures teach that as long as sinners struggle under the law, they will never have that peace of God which only comes to the justified. The imputation of sin is only removed when there is no law (Romans 5:13). This justifying peace is not through Moses but through the Lord Jesus Christ (Romans 5:1b). The question is, if we cannot be made just by the works of the law and justification is not of the law but something quite different, what is it?

Justification by a free gift
One thing is certain in this life. No one ever earned justification apart from Christ who earned it for us. Justification either comes as a gift or it does not come at all. Paul teaches clearly in Romans 5:15, 17:

> But not as the offence, so also is the free gift. For if through the offence of one many be dead, much more the grace of God, and the gift by grace, which is by one man, Jesus Christ hath abounded unto many. And not as it was by one that sinned, so is the gift: for the judgment was by one to condemnation, but the free gift is of many offences unto justification. For if by one man's offence death reigned by one; much more they which receive abundance of grace and the free gift of righteousness shall reign in life by one, Jesus Christ.

Here we are taught clearly by God's Word that though condemnation is a legal pronouncement of a sentence which we have deserved, justification is a free gift of grace which we have not deserved for two very sound reasons. 1. Nobody is justified by his legal behaviour because justification is not of the law 2. Justification is always given irrespective of the law through the venue of grace (Acts 13:39; Galatians 2:16; 3:11; 5:4 and the above references in Romans 5). Sinners do not have to pay for their salvation. They cannot. Justification is a gift of God.

Thus the gospel we preach is the gospel of gifts of grace not rewards for legal activities. Right at the beginning of his ministry to the Gentiles, Jesus, speaking to the woman of Samaria, tells us in John 4:10, "If thou knewest the gift of God, and who it is that saith to thee, Give me to drink; thou wouldest have asked of him, and he would have given thee living water." Jesus was obviously speaking to an elect woman here who could respond faithfully saying, "Sir, give me this water, that I thirst not, neither come hither to draw." Here we are reminded of Isaiah's glorious gospel call in chapter 55 to Christ's Bride as Christ's ambassador, saying, "Ho, every one that thirsteth, come ye to the waters, and he that hath no money; come ye, buy, and eat; yea come, buy wine and milk without money and without price." Christ's gospel call goes out to those who have nothing to bring Him but their debts and He promises them a gift which they could never afford.

Justification by ordination
When Paul preached at Antioch in Pisidia on two successive Sabbaths about being justified from all things by Christ and not Moses, he was speaking to a mixed audience of Jews and Gentiles about the prophecies concerning Christ and the salvation to be found in Him. This salvation, he taught, ensured justification. Thus justification is intricately tied up with the Person of Christ and His works. It is faith in the efficacy of this Christ-wrought justification that gives us peace with God (Romans 5:1a). Naturally, the questions immediately arises where does this faith come from? Is it a work of man or a work of God? Paul answered this question in his very first great sermon on justification with the words, "as many as were ordained to eternal life believed" (Acts 13:48). Here Paul was not coming up with anything new in God's Word. Even Isaiah in the old dispensation was given spiritual insight to see this. In chapter 6:12 we read, "Lord, thou wilt ordain peace for us: for thou also hast wrought all our works in us." Christ tells His sheep in John 15:16, "Ye have not chosen me, but I have chosen you, and ordained you, that ye should remain: that whatsoever ye shall ask of the Father in my name, he may give it you." That this ordination is not to a mere legal status which does not activate the person justified is clear from Ephesians 2:10, "For we are

Justification

his workmanship, created in Christ Jesus unto good works, which God hath before ordained that we should walk in them." This fact is difficult for very many Christians to accept as they are brought up in the traditions of works-righteousness and the idea that God only helps those who are able to help themselves. Indeed, it must be admitted that many of our present day evangelists and pastors would not dare to preach faith by ordination. But this is exactly how the New Testament saints preached. Paul, speaking of God's election, predestination and calling, tells us that the elect are called according to God's purpose and are predestinated to be conformed to the image of Christ. These elect sinners are called out of the world to be God's own special children and grace releases them from all the charges of the law. Paul can thus ask rhetorically, "Who shall lay any thing to the charge of God's elect? The answer is profoundly simple, "No one, because it is none other than God who has justified them and no one can bring any charges against God" (Romans 8:33).

Justification by adoption

The Old Testament introduces the Redeemer in His capacity as Mediator as 'The Everlasting Father' (Isaiah 9:6) and we read that His delight was in the children of God. In Isaiah 8:18 this Redeemer proclaims "Behold, I and the children whom the Lord hath given me are for signs and for wonders in Israel from the Lord of hosts, which dwelleth in mount Zion." This is repeated in Hebrews 2:13 as the testimony of Christ concerning the elect. Furthermore, we read in Titus 3:7 "That being justified by his grace, we should be made heirs according to the hope of eternal life." The elect children of God are put into the care of Christ to be redeemed from the bondage of the law and justified by faith (Galatians 3:24, 26; 4:5, 6). They are not such, however, by natural birth but by adoption. We read in Ephesians 1:4-6 that God chose His special children before the foundation of the world and predestined them to be adopted "by Jesus Christ to himself, according to the good pleasure of his will." We notice that this was all arranged and carried out in eternity and not time. Paul, in Romans 8:14-16, tells us that "as many as are led by the Spirit of God, they are the sons of God. For ye have not received the spirit of bondage again to fear; but ye have received the Spirit of adoption, whereby we cry,

Abba, Father. The Spirit itself beareth witness with our spirit that we are the children of God." These are the elect saints whom Paul says (v. 30) are the predestinated, called, justified and glorified. Obviously the justification which makes us heirs with God is not an abstract, theoretical mere start on a life of justification but it entails a continuing relationship with the Father through union with Christ, led by the Spirit. Throughout the remaining years of life, the justified child of God, fortified by the spirit, awaits the redemption that is synonymous with his adoption (v. 23). Thus, if we are justified by the faith of Christ, though our bodies are dead because of sin, the Spirit in us gives us life on the basis of Christ's righteousness and our union with Him and not our dead works. Any doctrine of justification preached which ignores this glorious fact is inadequate in instructing the sinner in righteousness. It is not presenting the entire call of the gospel to sinful man.

Justification by faith
Most Reformed Christians agree to the Biblical fact that we are justified by faith but the different explanations they give for this are legion. Most believe rightly that faith is a gift of God but conclude wrongly that God grants us justification after granting us faith. Sadly, many believe erroneously that God waits patiently until the sinner believes of his own accord and then rewards him with justification. For them, justification is always conditional and never decretal or absolute. These, however, are not the views of our first generation Reformers who rightly understood Scripture. The Bible teaches clearly that there is no faith in sinners unless they are first justified. God justifies His enemies and those who are ungodly. Galatians 3:8 tells us that God justifies the heathen through faith and we are obviously to understand this in keeping with Romans 4:5, "To him that worketh not, but believeth on him that justifieth the ungodly, his faith is counted for righteousness." This is the theme of the entire chapter of Romans 5 which tells us that Christ died for the ungodly (v. 6) and that this death for us was whilst we were yet sinners (vv. 7, 8). Indeed, this death did not occur whilst we were benevolent ungodly sinners capable of viewing Christ with a saving interest; it occurred "when we were enemies" of God. Yet it was then that God justified us and

Justification

reconciled us to Himself. Thus human faith cannot precede justification. But just as any righteousness we have is the righteousness of Christ in us, outworked in us by the Spirit according to the will of the Father, so our faith cannot be called human in any way. The saints in Revelation 14:12 are described as those who keep the commandments of God and have the faith of Jesus. This can only mean that they have a faith which is not of their own making but is the faith of the Lord Jesus Christ given to them. So, too, Christ says to the Pergamos church that they have held fast to His name and kept, not their own faith, but Christ's (Revelation 2:13) and, because of this, the Christian can say, "I live by the faith of the Son of God, who loved me, and gave himself for me" (Galatians 2:20).

Galatians is a wonderful epistle for spelling out the origin, outcome and goals of faith in very clear and precise terms. We read in Galatians 2:16:

> Knowing that a man is not justified by the works of the law, but by the faith of Jesus Christ, even we have believed in Jesus Christ, that we might be justified by the faith of Christ, and not by the works of the law: for by the works of the law shall no flesh be justified.

When, therefore, we read that Christ dwells in our hearts by faith (Ephesians 3:17), and that we have access to God by faith (Ephesians 3:12), it is Christ's faith which is meant, a faith which is ever working in our hearts, justifying[110] us and keeping us faithful. Every Christian's testimony is thus that of Paul, i.e. "that I might win Christ, And be found in him, not having mine own righteousness, which is of the law, but that which is through the faith of Christ, the righteousness which is of God by faith" (Philippians 3:8, 9). There is no faith, therefore, without the faith that Christ gives us, making us partakers of His faith. Hebrews 12:2 can thus rightly claim that the Christian's gaze must ever be "looking unto Jesus the author and finisher of our faith; who for the joy that was set before him endured the cross,

---

[110] I do not mean here that justification is an incomplete process but that justification entails God's faithfulness in keeping us eternally justified.

despising the shame, and is set down at the right hand of God." Justification thus entails not merely a legal, declarative act but it is the fulfilment of Christ's joy in us. Christ in us is our hope of glory, not some legal 'as if' status. There is nothing forensic or fictive about grace.

This does not mean, however, that the believer has not been given a personal faith which enables him to serve God in an individual way. We nowhere read that the sinner receives the full faith of Christ in this life. The weakness of the forensic theory is that it removes from justification the personal encounter between Christ and the Holy Spirit on one side and the believer on the other. In justification there is obviously a transforming work done here which goes far beyond a mere legal pronouncement on God's part. Luther saw this but Melanchthon constructed his system without due regard to this essential fact. The result is that justification is separated from its characteristics, contents and fruits. The believer is given an 'as if' faith to cope with an 'as if' justification. This would mean that no real justification or real faith becomes the believer's lot. Faith imputed, however, according to Scripture, must be a true faith which is actually given to the elect sinner. The upholding of this faith is then a divine communication from Christ's faith to that given the believer as an instrument of justification. It is not an idle faith but one activated by the Spirit and motivated by love (Galatians 5:5, 6). It is a medium by which the Spirit reveals to us our adoption and the way of holiness and sanctification. Indeed, faith is described as the fruit of the Spirit (Galatians 5:22) accompanied by love, joy, peace, longsuffering, gentleness and goodness. These gifts are complementary to justification and cannot be separated from it. Having said that, Romans 12:3 and 1 Corinthians 12:9 suggest that God does not give all His children the same measure of faith so we find even the Apostles begging Jesus to increase their faith (Luke 17:5). There is then, in the matter of Christ's faith which is given by measure to His sheep, a perpetual communication of righteousness as expressed in Romans 1:17, "For therein (the gospel) is the righteousness of God revealed from faith to faith: as it is written, The just shall live by faith." This could mean that God's faith is communicated to the portion of faith given to the individual believer or that through God's

Justification

righteous gospel the believer is enabled to grow from one degree of faith to another as he grows in grace and the knowledge of Jesus. Whichever explanation, the result is the same. However difficult it is to understand the meaning and outworking of the faith given in justification, it is obviously not a mere legal and forensic item but that which equips the believer to lead a life of righteous service within God's divine strategy for this world. Faith entails believing that the new man God makes of us is created in righteousness and true holiness (Ephesians 4:24) and also that the work God has begun in us will be perfected (Philippians 1:6).

Justification by forgiveness
Nowhere is forgiveness so linked with justification and set up in contrast to justification by the law as in Romans 3:20-26:

> Therefore by the deeds of the law there shall no flesh be justified in his sight: for by the law is the knowledge of sin. But now the righteousness of God without the law is manifested, being witnessed by the law and the prophets; Even the righteousness of God which is by faith of Jesus Christ unto all and upon all that believe: for there is no difference: For all have sinned, and come short of the glory of God; Being justified freely by his grace through the redemption that is in Christ Jesus: whom God hath set forth to be a propitiation through faith in his blood, to declare his righteousness for the remission of sins that are past, through the forbearance of God. To declare, I say, at this time his righteousness: that he might be just, and the justifier of him which believeth in Jesus.

Paul thus spoke of justification and the forgiveness of sins in the same breath. These are inseparable factors in salvation. You cannot have one without the other (Acts 13:38-41). The clear message of Paul is that justification is a work of God which brings with it the forgiveness of sins. Indeed, throughout Paul's teaching in Romans 5, we find that it is his justification through the gift of forgiveness which characterises the saved sinner. This gift is placed as the antonym of condemnation by the law. A further contrast of the forensic condemnation through the Mosaic law on the one side with justification by grace on the other is seen in the continuation of Romans 5:17 quoted above concerning the gift of justification. We read on in verse 18, "Therefore as by the offence of one judgment came upon all men to condemnation; even so by the righteousness of one the free gift came upon all men unto justification." This shows that what is of law cannot be of grace. Again, Paul hammers this truth home in the previous chapter when he links the justifying of the ungodly with the forgiveness and non-imputation of sin (4:5 ff.). In Romans 6:17 ff., Paul outlines that there is no righteousness (justification) possible for those who are the servants of sin but those who have been freed from sin and made righteous in Christ, "ye have your fruit unto holiness, and the end everlasting life." Here, Paul is saying that justification does not entail being declared righteous and then becoming holy through sincere obedience but that holy fruit and eternal life are the ingredients of that righteousness given us in Christ. Justification thus entails "Being filled with the fruits of righteousness, which are by Jesus Christ, unto the glory and praise of God" (Philippians 1:11).

Justification by the Spirit

When Paul in Romans 8 outlines the way Christ fulfilled the righteousness of the law on our behalf, he says, "There is therefore now no condemnation to them which are in Christ Jesus, who walk not after the flesh, but after the Spirit. For the law of the Spirit of life in Christ Jesus hath made me free from the law of sin and death (vv. 1, 2). Thus Paul relates justification directly to the quickening work of the Spirit. In 1 Timothy 3:16 when referring to the work of God the Father, Son and Holy Spirit in salvation, Paul speaks of Christ's justifying act of redemption on behalf of the elect sinner as a justification in the Spirit. Just as the Spirit demonstrated Christ to be the Just One in His incarnation, Paul argues, so he demonstrates the elect sinners' justification before angels and men, made possible, derived and worked out through Christ's justifying and vicarious sacrifice. Thus we read in Romans 8:9 ff., "Now if any man have not

Justification

the Spirit of Christ, he is none of his. And if Christ be in you, the body is dead because of sin; but the Spirit is life because of righteousness. But if the Spirit of him that raised up Jesus from the dead dwell in you, he that raised up Christ from the dead shall also quicken your mortal bodies by his Spirit that dwelleth in you." Furthermore, in those adopted children of God in whom the Spirit works in a justifying way, we find fruits of goodness, righteousness and truth in the believer (Ephesians 5:9). So, again we see that justification is not a mere 'as if' righteousness of a mere forensic kind, but a fitting out to live a productive life of justification in the Spirit. Indeed, "as many as are led by the Spirit of God, they are the sons of God" (Romans 8:14). In other words, being led by the Spirit is as essential to justification as being convicted and converted by the Spirit.

Justification by imputation

The Christian doctrine of imputation is summed up in Romans 5:19 in the words, "For as by one man's disobedience many were made sinners, so by the obedience of one shall many be made righteous." The argument is that though death came on all men because of Adam's sin, those "which receive abundance of grace and of the gift of righteousness shall reign in life by one, Jesus Christ" (5:17). Paul explains that Christ has made this possible by not only fulfilling the law on our behalf but also by bearing our punishments for not fulfilling it. Christ thus made atonement for our sins and God was satisfied with His Son's way of reconciling sinners back to God and accepted the sacrifice. God thus, when He views His elect, views them as being in union with Christ and His Bride. Because Christ's righteousness was placed in lieu of the elect sinners who belong to Him, God now judges those with Him as righteous. The sinner is in union with Christ as His Bride, indeed, as His Body, and as such adopted by the Father and Christ and His Spirit are said to indwell the believer, leading him on to ways of righteousness which will ultimately, after the believer's glorification in Heaven, produce a fully perfect and righteous being. Justification therefore has a passive and active side. The elect believer is accounted justified because of what the Father, Son and Holy Ghost have done for him and is being made just by what God is doing in Him. Writing of Abraham in Romans 4,

Paul explains that justification by faith imputed to Abraham by God on behalf of His Son is illustrative of God's covenant dealings with all to whom righteousness is imputed. Abraham was not justified by works (v. 2). Therefore God was not in debt to him to make him just (v. 4). The way God made Abraham just was to forgive him his iniquities and cover his sins (v. 7). This was purely and simply a work of grace. The result was that Abraham was able to accept the promises of God and given the grace to give all the glory to God and remain strong in the faith. Chapter 5 continues this account, saying that through such an imputation of righteousness the ungodly (4:5) receive access by faith into God's grace (5:2). This faith given is so strong, fostered by the love of God in the believer's heart that he is enabled to go through tribulations (v. 3). This teaches the believer patience and hope as he sees God working out His purpose in his life.

The weakness of the Melanchthonian theory of a mere forensic imputation is that it reduces the work of Christ on behalf of the individual elect sinner to a mere external, impersonal formality. A theory of justification through the imputed righteousness of Christ which argues away the Good Shepherd's personal relationship to His sheep in the justifying process has no basis in Scripture. Obviously the righteousness which is given the elect sinner is Christ's righteousness and equally obvious is that this is given him through no merits of his own.

Yet this righteousness is not a mere legal mechanism. It is not even a catalyst in the process of the sinner becoming holy which helps that process but never becomes an actual part of it. The imputation of Christ's righteousness to the sinner is only made possible through the personal encounter of the sinner with Christ. It is the natural outcome of the elect sinner being put in union with his Saviour. Justified sinners are made acceptable to the Beloved One (Ephesians 1:6). Such elect children of God are then described as holy and beloved themselves (Colossians 3:12). It is this personal encounter which changes the sinner and not a mere formal declaration of being considered just. Calvin's teaching could not be more opposite to Melanchthon's. He criticises most strongly the 'pestilential philosophers' and 'semi-papists' in the churches who deny this dynamic link. For him, the righteous Christ is always in the believer.

Justification

Of his Saviour Calvin says, "We expect salvation from him – not because he stands aloof from us, but because ingrafting us into his body, he not only makes us partakers of all his benefits, but also of himself ... He tells us that the condemnation which we of ourselves deserve is annihilated by the salvation of Christ; and to confirm this he employs the argument to which I have referred – viz. that Christ is not external to us, but dwells in us; and not only unites us to himself by an undivided bond of fellowship, but by a wondrous communion brings us daily into closer connection, until he becomes altogether one with us."[111]

Summing up

Calvin's words could not be a better summary of the entire scope of justification. The doctrine has nothing to do with a Christ who is afar off, a Father who merely makes legal declarations and a Spirit who is conspicuous by His absence in the believer. Justification means that God is nigh. Indeed, it means that Christ our Head has taken command of our destination and His Spirit indwells us, witnessing to our spirit that we are the children of God. Justification cannot be separated from its blessings which God foreordained for us before ever the world was. The Biblical doctrine of justification is that God equips His adopted children for eternity, from eternity. Thus, one cannot talk about justification without taking into account every merciful aspect of salvation by which God in Christ by the Spirit has reconciled us to Himself. This is the glorious gospel that we are to bring as the best good news possible to the world. Ours is not the gospel of pessimism or scepticism which tells sinners that Christ has died for nobody in particular, and justification is for any who will come and get it. Justification is for those led by the Spirit who see their total lack of righteousness and are persuaded in their hearts and consciences that their only hope for eternity is to taste and see that the Lord is good and that His righteous grace is sufficient for all who come to Him. It is to such people that Christ says, "Cast thy burden upon the Lord for He shall sustain thee: he shall never suffer the righteous to be moved (Psalm 55:22).

---

[111] *Institutes*, Book III, Chapter II, 24.

go *Topical*

Index of Scripture Verses

Justification

Justification

go *Topical*

General Index

Justification

Calvinism (Calvinist), 11, 22-25, 29, 34 fn., 63, 73-75
Cameron, John, 20
Charles II, 55, 87
Clifford, Alan, 20
Comrie, Alexander, 81
Congregationalism, 55
Cotton, John, 27
Coverdale, Miles, 8, 47 fn., 77, 77 fn.
Crampton, W. Gary, 11, 12, 23
Cranmer, Thomas, 33 fn., 75
Cremer, Hermann, 41, 41 fn.
Crisp, Tobias, 13
Cromwell, Oliver, 55, 59
D'Anvers, Colonel, 59
Daniel, Curt, 34 fn.
Davenant, John, Bishop, 20, 20 fn.
Davis, Donald, G., 22
De Pierre, François, 23
den Dulk Christian Foundation, 87
Dort, Synod of, 20
Dort, Canon of, 19, 82 fn.
Dutch Confession of Faith, 82
Dutch Reformed Liturgy, 82
Dutch States, 88, 89
Eastern Europe, 89
Edwards, Jonathan, Sen., 27
Eliot, John, 89
Elizabethan Settlement, 25
England, Church of, 19, 51, 59
Eveson, Philip, 58 fn.
Faukel, Herman, 82, 83
Ferguson, Sinclair, 23 fn.
Fetter Lane Congregation Church, 55
Finney, Charles, 8
Finneyism, 66
Fisher, G. P., 23
Fleming, Bishop, 7
Fowler, Christopher, 64
Fowler, Edward, 59-61
Franeker University, 87
Fuller, Andrew, 12, 13, 87 fn.
Fuller, Morris, 20

Justification

www.ingramcontent.com/pod-product-compliance
Lightning Source LLC
Chambersburg PA
CBHW020457100426
42812CB00024B/2695